So
Sorry
for
Your
Loss

Also by Dina Gachman:

Brokenomics: 50 Ways to Live the Dream on a Dime

So Sorry for Your Loss

How I Learned to Live with Grief, and Other Grave Concerns

Dina Gachman

UNION
SQUARE
& CO.

NEW YORK

**UNION
SQUARE
& CO.**

NEW YORK

UNION SQUARE & CO. and the distinctive Union Square & Co. logo
are trademarks of Sterling Publishing Co., Inc.

Union Square & Co., LLC, is a subsidiary of Sterling Publishing Co., Inc.

The portions in this book that are memoir reflect the author's present
recollections of experiences over time. Throughout the book, a few names
have been changed, either at the request of the person quoted or to protect
the privacy of the people in the story.

ISBN 978-1-4549-4760-8 (paperback)

ISBN 978-1-4549-4761-5 (ebook)

For information about custom editions, special sales, and premium
purchases, please contact specialsales@unionsquareandco.com.

Printed in Canada

2   4   6   8   10   9   7   5   3   1

unionsquareandco.com

Cover Photo by Sarah Jun

For Mom and Jackie.
And for Dad, Amy, and Kathryn. My lion pride.

Contents

Ah, grief, I should not treat you
like a homeless dog
who comes to the back door
for a crust, for a meatless bone.
I should trust you.

—Denise Levertov, "Talking to Grief"

Introduction

For years, my mom would say, "One day you'll write a book about Jackie." Neither of us could have imagined it would be this book, a story of loss. My mom hadn't yet been diagnosed with stage IV colon cancer, and my little sister Jackie was still managing to get herself intermittently sober, between increasingly frequent stints in and out of detoxes and rehabs. I think my mom wanted me to write Jackie's story so that she wasn't dismissed, as so many alcoholics are, as somehow weak or unworthy of love. I wish this could be about my sister's "triumph" over her addictions and my mom "beating" cancer. I wish both of them could read it, but they can't. They're gone, and I, like so many others, live with those losses every single day.

Another one of my mother's firmly held beliefs was this: "Honey, sometimes you just have to laugh." She didn't mean laugh while I was watching something objectively funny, like Meg Stalter TikToks or videos of pugs dressed as Baby Yoda. My mom was a fierce advocate for the cause of finding humor in the darkest of times. Over the years, I've adopted this belief as my own. It's become especially helpful in recent years, when I've had to process living a life without her, and without my sister.

Learning to live with deep grief has changed my life. I don't walk around in a black lace veil and weep throughout the day (well, not every day). I haven't covered the mirrors or stopped the clocks, as they did in the Victorian era. Still, even if I'm at a park with my son, or out with friends, that veil is always there in some form. Accepting that fact, and figuring out how to manage the emotions and thoughts that come with it, has been the most difficult part of this journey. If you've experienced loss, whether recently or years ago, you probably know all too well that living with grief becomes an ongoing, maybe even lifelong tug-of-war. Hopefully, eventually, it becomes less of a battle, and more of a gentle push and pull. But that takes time.

In a 2019 study about grief and loss, 53 percent of people surveyed said they had met someone who assumed their grief should have an end date. Of that group, 58 percent said they felt pressured to "recover" from grief within three months. If you're grieving the loss of a favorite pair of shoes, maybe, but a person? Even an animal? Someone you love deeply, and who you now find yourself living without? The day you stop grieving is the day you stop loving, and, for better or worse, that day will never come. That doesn't mean the initial crush of pain will remain forever. The pain transforms, each day, each year.

Renowned grief researcher and author Pauline Boss writes in her book *The Myth of Closure*, "Continuing to use the term 'closure' perpetuates the myth that losses and grief have a prescribed time for ending—or never starting—and that it's emotionally healthier to close the door on suffering than to face it and learn to live with it."

In the moments after finding out that my mom and then my sister had died, I couldn't understand that over time, my relationship with each of them would not actually end, but that it would evolve, and I would adapt and find ways to keep them in my life. I have no control over what has happened, so instead of waiting for some imaginary day when I'll find "closure," I ultimately accepted that my love for them, my grief, would become part of me, instead of something I had to conquer.

When Jackie died unexpectedly, in the winter of 2021, less than three years after my mom passed away, I had read my share of grief books, many of which I cherished for their ability to make me feel less alone in my pain. Eventually, I longed for a book about grief that would also allow me to, if not laugh, then at least crack a smile, or just feel a little lighter, and lift some of the heaviness I carried. Humor is an ancient survival tool, as crucial as the ability to outrun a predator or spear a woolly mammoth. Many archeologists believe early humans used torches to separate a woolly mammoth from the herd before steering it into a trap, which is a fact I just learned because I do not want people coming after *me* with torches and yelling, "Humans didn't spear woolly mammoths, you fool!" The point is, as my mother knew so well, humor, like traps and spears, has helped humans endure for centuries, and although I understand that funerals are not prime time for punch lines, and that you are not always going to be in the mood to laugh, it can help. It helps me tremendously.

I'm telling my story, and sharing the insights of others in this book, not because I have a simple plan for "getting over" grief or because I discovered a magic formula to move on with life after loss. I don't have any handy slogans to Band-Aid your sorrow. We're not living in the cinematic world of *Eternal Sunshine of the Spotless Mind*, where you can pay a team of pseudo-scientists to erase painful memories from your brain. I've just tried my best to learn to live with grief. That's all you can do, and it's no small thing. That's the push and pull that becomes part of everyday life.

It still sometimes surprises me that this is my reality. As I write this, it has been nearly four years since my mom died. Her clothes still hang in her closet. Her perfume sits on the bathroom counter. Some people might advise us to toss my mom's Tom Ford Black Orchid Eau de Parfum or her favorite petal pink silk shirt because it's unhealthy to keep them around, but we aren't ready to get rid of the reminders, not yet. For now, I find it comforting to visit my dad and see her jewelry and shoes, and so do my sisters. We are not ready to part with her things, even several years out. If purging someone's possessions helps you, do it. Burn them in a bonfire and set the ashes out to sea. No matter how you choose to grapple with it, grief gets into your bones. It's not an easy state of being to settle into, but it can be a meaningful one.

I hope the stories in this book bring comfort when you need it, laughter when you're feeling low, and a little bit of peace when the moment feels insurmountable. We can't rewind time, or have our memories erased, as they do in the movies, but we can try, every single day, to live with this. We can attempt to let it propel us, instead of allowing it to tug us back.

Chapter 1
This Is Not a Detour

The second phone call that launched me into deep grief happened on a Monday night. It was March 1, 2021, and our plane had just touched down in Austin. I was with my husband Jerett and our three-year-old son Cole, coming back from visiting my in-laws in Florida. If you've ever flown with a kid, maybe you can imagine my state of mind at that moment: frazzled, tense, and teetering on the edge of releasing a bloodcurdling scream. My hair was a tumbleweed and I was covered in half-eaten snacks.

Adding to my stress was the fact that, before our plane took off that day, I knew my sister Jackie was in trouble. She was so often in trouble, in and out of detoxes and rehabs, picked up by ambulances after being found on lawns or sidewalks by her kind neighbors in Queens, who were two married ex-cops who had probably seen their share of people passed out all over New York. I never met those neighbors, but I talked to them on the phone, listening as they explained that she was drunk again. Incoherent again. On her way back to detox, yet again. I would thank these strangers for doing what I could not, from so far across the country. This type of scenario happened so many times over the years, with different neighbors or friends or random acquaintances of Jackie's, that I cannot begin to count. Even so, she always managed to pull through, at least for a little while. I used to joke with my other sisters, Amy and Kathryn, that Jackie would outlive us all. She had nine lives, like a cat. It was our way of convincing each other, and ourselves, that she'd be okay.

This time around, while I was on that trip with my in-laws in Florida, Jackie had been missing for a few days, after nearly a year of sobriety. I was so relieved that she had finally gotten sober again right as the pandemic hit New York. During the winter of 2020, imagining her wandering through the streets and subways not sober, maskless, scared me.

Whenever Jackie disappeared in the past, it was usually a day or two, but she would always, without fail, contact our dad. She told him everything, and he always listened, never judging or scolding her, always trying his best to understand and encouraging her to get help. This time even he hadn't heard from her and neither had her husband, Niall. Thankfully, the morning of my flight back to Austin, we finally got a call from the police, saying they had found her in a motel in a small Colorado town, where she and Niall had recently moved to escape the chaos of New York and start a new life. When my plane landed back home in Austin, that's all I knew: They had found my sister. I figured the next call would be from my dad telling me that Jackie was back in detox. He would give me the number of the hospital so I could call her and tell her I loved her, and to please get help, again.

As the plane moved toward the gate, I brushed away some stray Cheerios and checked my phone. I saw a text from Amy:

I can't believe this is real.

"I need to call Amy," I told Jerett. My heart constricted, or at least it felt like it constricted. If you think that's dramatic, the Old English word for grief, *heartsarnes*, means soreness of the heart. Takotsubo cardiomyopathy, a legitimate medical condition, is a temporary weakening of the heart's main pumping chamber, which can make you feel like you're having a heart attack. It's also called broken-heart syndrome, and clinically referred to as stress cardiomyopathy. Some experts suggest that it is caused by a surge of hormones associated with the fight-or-flight instinct, such as adrenaline. Anyone who has experienced the sledgehammer of grief understands that your chest actually hurts. The physical pain can be shocking, the way our bodies process our emotions, pulverizing us, pinning us to that exact moment in time. I had felt this pain before. Like broken-heart syndrome, grief is not a simple thing to diagnose, but I recognized that heart-pounding dizziness when it came for me again.

"Why don't you wait to call Amy until we get home?"

There was nothing casual about the way Jerett said this. His tone was tentative, a little too cautious. I didn't even have to look over at him to realize that he knew something I did not. As Jerett tried to keep Cole from leapfrogging out of our seats while we waited for people to deplane, I stared at Amy's text:

I can't believe this is real.

All the forces in the world could not have stopped me from dialing Amy's number. So I did.

"You can't believe what's real?" I asked before she could say hello. "The police said they found her this morning, right?" I knew, in my bones, what she meant, and what she couldn't believe. I just wanted so badly to be wrong. I wanted nine lives for Jackie, ten, as many as it took.

Through tears, Amy explained that she and my dad and Kathryn had texted Jerett, telling him the news but begging him to keep it from me until we got home. Amy was so distraught that she forgot their pledge and texted anyway. We had been telling each other everything practically since the day she was born and I was three years old, and that's a tough habit to break. The initial thought was that they didn't want me to hear this news on an airplane, as if there is any good place to discover that your sister has died. Would a tropical beach with a mai tai in hand have lessened the blow? Maybe if I'd been on top of the Eiffel Tower at sunset, it wouldn't have hurt as much? A claustrophobic plane with a feral three-year-old wasn't ideal, but no place is. Amy said that they had found Jackie, but that hours later, they called back and told my dad, while he was at dinner with a friend, that his daughter, my sister, the third of his four girls, was gone.

"When I got the call from the police officer, I didn't want to believe what he said," my dad told me when I later asked about that night. "My heart was pounding so much, I thought I was going to have a heart attack."

Earlier that day, Kathryn heard from an employee at the motel that Jackie had checked out. They weren't supposed to give out that kind of information, but Kathryn begged, pleaded, and explained the situation. So that's all we knew—Jackie wasn't there anymore. She'd supposedly gotten into a fight with Niall and left their apartment a few days before, and somehow wound up in this motel. When they told us Jackie had left, we thought maybe she'd gone to detox again, and that we'd get a call from her soon. That never happened, though. The police found her at the motel, but it took all day for them to investigate or do whatever they needed to do, and then hours later my dad got that awful call.

"It was a terrible night," my dad said. "I remember thinking, *How am I going to process this?* After going through the grief of losing your mom, I was starting to get my emotions in check, as much as you can, I guess, and then this happened. I remember wondering how I was going to make it through, like how much can one person take in two or three years? I wanted it not to be true. I understood what the police officer said, but I was in a fog. It just knocks your emotions out of whack."

In the weeks to come, I would call that small-town police department a few times, imagining a small, musty detective's office with files and papers scattered about, like a grainy 1970s film, or, for some reason, like the detective office in Spike Lee's *Blackkklansman*. I imagined Jackie's file tossed on a desk, too far away for me to touch. I left messages, and missed call-backs, but I never got answers. Jackie was just another body to them. To me, she was the baby sister who wanted to sleep in my bed every night when we were young. The one who was so sensitive and empathetic that as a kid she asked me to write letters for her, addressed to Jane Goodall, asking Dame Jane how Jackie Gachman, a six-year-old in Texas, could help save the chimpanzees. She was the teenager and then the woman who was made fun of for her learning differences and eccentric ways, and who went through hell fighting addiction for the majority of her short life. Her bone-dry sense of humor was a gift. She had an old Hollywood—type beauty, like Hedy Lamarr or Elizabeth Taylor, and her love for David Bowie was legendary. The people who found her would never know any of that, though.

As soon as I heard that Jackie was gone, I told Amy I couldn't talk. Or maybe I mumbled some indecipherable syllables. It's hard to say. I do remember that my phone tumbled out of my hand. Normally, seeing my phone lying on the floor of an airplane during a pandemic, I would have panic-lunged for the hand sanitizer and Clorox wipes, but I couldn't move. I felt nothing, and everything at once. As we waited for our turn to exit the plane, I lowered my head and squeezed my eyes shut to try to control the emotions that were threatening to break the surface and roar to life. I didn't care about the strangers surrounding me, but I knew what was coming and I didn't want to scare my son. Jerett took my hand, I kept my head bowed, and I tried, as hard as I could, to breathe.

When we got home and put Cole to bed, I cried myself to sleep. I was trying to come to terms not just with the reality that my sister was gone, but that my dad and my other two sisters and I were about to do all of this again. Just when we were starting to feel almost halfway settled into our new reality, so soon after losing my mom, grief unexpectedly surged back.

One thing I have learned to be true is that death doesn't discriminate, and neither does grief. They are equal opportunity assholes, and they induct all of us into their crappy club at some point, whether we like it or not.

There isn't a "good" kind of loss, but maybe there is a difference between losing a beloved grandparent who is ninety-five years old or a math teacher who died peacefully in their sleep at eighty, and losing a parent to cancer, or losing a sibling or child or best friend too young. I was painfully sad when each of my four grandparents passed away. I miss them every day. But the process of learning to live with that grief had nothing on learning to live with the loss of my mom at sixty-eight, and my sister at just forty. That kind of loss changes everything, even, many scientists believe, the wiring of your brain.

Grief therapist Ajita Robinson says she's had both personal and professional experience with this phenomenon of grief impacting the way the brain functions. She initially went to law school with the goal of working with Black youth and their families, to help mitigate their involvement in the legal system. Law school was a way for her to hide from her own grief, which stemmed from childhood trauma due to physical and emotional abuse, as well as witnessing community violence at a young age.

"I did everything I could not to be a grief counselor," Robinson says. "A major reason I ran from grief work is that I hadn't ever sat and processed my own grief. I didn't feel equipped, emotionally, to bear witness to the suffering of others. I hadn't experienced the healing aspect of grief therapy because I had never received the opportunity to heal."

She took some elective courses in grief and trauma and, with the help of a mentor, she embraced her true calling, left law, and did the personal work to confront her own emotions.

Robinson says the emotional processing of grief can be a "psychological injury" that can affect short- and long-term memory, word recall, emotional processing, and the ability to retain new information. She says this can be especially common with cumulative or prolonged grief, and she tells people not to make big decisions in the immediate aftermath of loss. It took her years to get to a place where she could make major decisions about her career or her life choices. If she were younger, and hadn't gotten the help she needed to work through her grief, those decisions would have been nearly impossible to make.

This type of response isn't just reserved for parents or siblings or children. It can also happen when a beloved grandparent passes away or, possibly, a beloved eighty-year-old math teacher.

So maybe by assuming that the loss of a grandparent hurts less than the loss of a parent or sibling, I'm actually being an equal opportunity ageist. Maybe your grandmother raised you and made you the person you are today, or your grandfather was the most important person in your life. What about the fact that, as of December 2021, an estimated 75 percent of people who had died of Covid in the United States were sixty-four years old or older? That's a generation of grandparents, with children and grandchildren and friends who mourn them. It's pretty insulting to all grandparents and elders to say that their deaths are just a little less painful. I know my paternal grandfather would have played golf and had martini lunches until he was 350 years old if he had the choice. The man loved life. He didn't have a choice, though. None of us do.

Whether someone passes away suddenly at a young age or takes their final bow at nearly a hundred years old, like beloved Betty White, one of the rudest things you can say to someone—or *about* someone—is probably, "Well, they lived a long life!" Even if they were 102 years old, they were *alive*, and then, suddenly, they weren't. Maybe they wanted a few more years to enjoy tacos and game shows and people-watching on the porch. Maybe they were running marathons at ninety-five years old and felt like they still had an Iron Man race or two in them. "They lived a long life" is one of those things we say when we don't know what else to say. Like so many things we utter in the face of grief, we might mean well, but until you've been inducted into this club-with-zero-perks, you don't realize that there are so many better things to say, and ways to say them.

Take "So sorry for your loss." Everyone tweets it and writes it on Facebook threads and texts it and mumbles it at funerals. When I saw it or heard it in the months following my mom's death, it felt like go-to sympathy. A zero-drama sentiment. I get why people say it—they're afraid to upset the person who is already distraught. But really, we are so upset already that someone could say, "That SUCKS. I am sorry. HOW HORRIBLE" and we would probably not be phased. Trust me, we know it's horrible. We will not break if people say, "What a tragedy." We may break down in tears, but we won't break. At first, the safe condolences bothered me, and then they full-on angered me. I wanted someone to say THIS IS HELL ON EARTH so that I could yell back I KNOW IT IS, THANK YOU FOR UNDERSTANDING! It took time to go from wanting to scream every time I heard "My sympathies" or "So sorry for your loss" to deeply appreciating those words. Eventually, I learned that the worst thing you can say is nothing, so simply saying, "I'm sorry" or "So sorry for your loss" can mean everything to someone in pain.

"The niceties of grief can be difficult to hear," says Marian Mankin, program director at the Houston bereavement center Bo's Place, where my dad sought counseling. She mentions the phrase "God wouldn't give you more than you can handle" as one that can trigger pain or anger in the bereaved. Mankin uses an exercise called "Helpful, Not Helpful," where people can talk about the things that actually help them in their grief, and the things that are triggering. "There is a social awkwardness that happens because we are a very grief-avoidant culture," Mankin says. "So people look to what is commonly said, even though it might not convey anything about the person who died."

I spent most of my life not knowing what to say in the face of grief. One of my closest friends, Rachel, lost her older brother to cancer when he was in high school and she was still a preteen, years before I met her. When this huge and

Helpful	Not Helpful
I'm so sorry	They're in a better place
I'm here for you	God won't give you more than you can handle
Take all the time you need	Time heals all wounds
I dropped some lasagna at your door	What can I do? What can I bring? (aka Don't make us think)
I loved them so much	At least they're not suffering anymore
You don't have to talk	So how did it happen???
Man, they were funny	They lived a long life
I can't imagine what you're going through	I know EXACTLY how you feel
Take care of yourself	When are you coming back to work, because your workload is piling up by the hour
My heart aches for you	What time is the funeral and what's the address? What are you wearing? Is there parking? Will there be food?
What a tragedy, this is so unfair	★ Silence ★ (ANYTHING IS BETTER THAN SILENCE)

important part of her life came to light, I remember feeling tongue-tied. I had no words to bridge the divide between us. I probably said, "I'm so sorry," and then moved on to another topic. Not because I didn't care, but because the subject was so overwhelming and I was afraid to upset her. I had lost grandparents, but it felt like her brother's death was somehow different. If Rachel wasn't talking about it, neither would I. For years, her brother would occasionally come up in conversation—maybe her mom or dad would post a photo of him, or a story would be told that he was part of—but we never really went there. We stayed on the surface, or I did. I *was* so sorry for her loss, but I was terrified to go deeper, and scared to churn things up.

Fast-forward twenty years into our friendship, and in May 2015, five weeks before my wedding, I got a call from my dad telling me that my mom had stage IV colon cancer. I remember my phone dropping out of my hand at the end of that conversation, too, just as it would a few years later on that airplane. I guess that's my initial reflex when it comes to grief—literally losing my grip.

When I got the news, Rachel was one of the first people I reached out to. The way we spoke about my mom and about her brother, from that day forward, was different. Grief isn't a language you learn slowly. There is no Duolingo for this. When it happens, it's as if a secret linguistic portal rips open and suddenly there you are, with an entirely new way of communicating and existing in the world. You have a psychic secret handshake with others who've gone through painful loss. I'm not as scared to ask Rachel questions anymore, because I know that grief isn't something you should wrap up and store away, like a fragile glass figurine. It will, and should, become part of you. Maybe even a tough, unbreakable part of you. But that realization did not happen on day one. On day one, I tried to tuck my feelings away, because I had a wedding shower to go to.

Learning about my mom's diagnosis was the beginning of deep grief for me, even though she fought (yes, fought) for nearly four years after that day. Many people think there are supposed to be five or seven or even twelve "stages" of grief, but the most common stages people seem to know are Denial, Anger, Bargaining, Depression, and Acceptance. Those stages were actually identified as a common journey for people who were dying, not for those left behind, but over time they became mistakenly viewed as the stages of grief. These stages were created by famed psychiatrist and researcher Elisabeth Kübler-Ross, in her book *On Death and Dying*. Later in her life, Kübler-Ross expressed regret that the five stages had been misinterpreted and misrepresented in pop culture for so long. I'm no psychologist or psychiatrist, but I would agree with her and say the emotions that accompany loss can't really be counted, or placed in any neat and tidy order. Sometimes we just want and need to give order to the chaos, though.

"With grief there is no single process," says Dr. Damita Sunwolf LaRue, a Chicago-based psychologist who specializes in grief and loss. LaRue grew up in Texas, and she's a tribal citizen of the Cherokee Nation. Her earliest teacher was her grandmother, a medicine woman named Hazel LaRue DeWing. LaRue incorporates her Cherokee heritage into her practice and says that sometimes, what people truly need is a "witness to their story," and that comes from a culture focused on interconnectedness. "For me, that is a huge connection to who I am as an Indian," she says. "The communal piece is the most healing. The reality is that sitting with someone in the pain and being fully present is the biggest gift you can give. In Indian culture we are storytellers, and people need to tell their story. My job is to make sure they're safe while telling their story, and to help them with coping skills."

LaRue told me that the "average American" believes they have to go through the five stages of grief, and she tries to help them understand that those stages are misconceptions. "Often, when people come to me, their first question is: *Am I doing it right?* The reality is, there is no 'right' way to do grief."

That's comforting, because on the day I found out about my mom's diagnosis, I'm pretty sure I skipped Denial and Anger and went straight to Bargaining.

When I hung up after talking to my parents, the last thing in the world I felt like doing was going to a party, in my honor, to celebrate an event that I wasn't even sure I'd end up having. I wanted to crawl into bed and pull the covers over my head. I wanted to fly home to Texas and hug my mom. I wanted to rewind time, and stay there. Instead, I went into the bathroom and started putting on mascara. My movements were robotic, the opposite of the elegant flourishes you see models in ads using to whip on their Maybelline Great Lash before they jeté into the night wearing sequined miniskirts. My only flourish was my ability to apply mascara while weeping. As I half-attempted to make myself look semi-presentable for a wedding shower that now sounded like torture, the bargaining began.

"God? Or the Universe? What do you want from me?
WHAT DO I NEED TO DO TO MAKE THIS GO AWAY?"

I'm not extremely religious, but I do talk to *someone* out there in the universe. Or maybe I'm talking to THE UNIVERSE? Who knows? I guess I felt that someone might be willing to strike a deal with me. Maybe they were reasonable and open to compromise? No such luck, though. All I got was silence. From my bathroom window in the Eagle Rock neighborhood of Los Angeles, where we lived at the time, I could see the traffic creeping along the 210 freeway. People were going to work or school. The world was still moving outside, even though my world inside that house felt like it had stopped still, as if I were looking out at a daily life that

I was suddenly separated from. With that one phone call, everything I knew, or thought I knew, had changed.

I had a choice. I could cancel the shower and stay home and cry my mascara off and curse the universe, which I knew people would understand. Or I could finish putting on the stupid makeup, get in the car and onto that packed freeway, and go. My husband's coworkers had put so much effort into the shower, and my mom always advised us to live by the Elizabeth Taylor mantra of "Put on some lipstick, pour yourself a drink, and pull yourself together." So I did. I didn't pour myself a drink, since it was nine in the morning, but I did put on lipstick and I sort of pulled myself together. Or so I thought.

I burst into tears about ten minutes into the shower. I don't remember if something in particular set me off, or if it was everything at once. Maybe it was the knowledge that this huge moment in my life was coming, I was having a wedding, and I needed my mom to be by my side, now more than ever. If she couldn't be there, how could I go through with it? People awkwardly ate some cake, but none of the games were played. When it became clear that my crying wasn't going to stop unless someone knocked me out with a 2x4, the guests slowly shuffled away and went back to work. Soon the only people left in the room were myself, Jerett, and Lauren, his coworker and friend who threw the shower. After I apologized for ruining her party, Lauren gently told me that her grandfather had been diagnosed with cancer years before.

"You have a long road ahead of you," Lauren said.

What the hell? I didn't have a long road ahead. This would all be over in a few months or at most one year, and we would throw a "Mom beat cancer party" and go on with our lives. This would not be a long road; it would be a quick detour. A stint. A mere blink in the whole scheme of things. Lauren spent months planning this wedding shower and crafting cute and thoughtful decorations and putting together a slideshow with childhood photos of me and Jerett that she had surreptitiously acquired from our parents, but, in that moment, she was my archnemesis.

I went from Bargaining to Denial, with a large dose of Anger, in the course of just a few hours.

Imagining alternate realities (and pretending that we didn't have a "long road" ahead) became a way for me to cope as soon as I got the call about my mom's diagnosis, and I still, on occasion, think *What if?* What if she'd gotten a colonoscopy at fifty or sixty, instead of sixty-five? What if it was treatable? What if none of it ever happened and I could pick up the phone and call her right now? It's hard to keep your mind from going there, even years after the loss. Joan Didion wrote about creating alternate realities in *The Year of Magical Thinking*, like keeping her husband's shoes around even after his death, just in case, somehow, in some yearned-for alternate universe, he came back to her. We still have my mom's clothes, shoes, and jewelry in her closet, not because we think she'll walk through the front door and ask where her favorite cardigan is, but because, in some sense, we're not ready to part with those reminders of her existence, even several years later. I know she's gone forever, but the finality of going through her things is still too much.

"There were no faint traces about dead, no pencil marks," Didion wrote. It's the only line in her beautiful book that I underlined, once I got the courage to read it several months after my mom's death. The whole book is worth underlining, but, for me, this one spare sentence stands out. Accepting the finality of death is a painful step in the process of learning to ache for someone forever, while allowing yourself to experience life, and moments of joy, even as you hurt.

Along this rocky pathway through grief I've read the Zen sayings and the comforting quotes about death being a part of life. I've had to stop myself from texting my mom about a piece of celebrity gossip I know she'd love when I remember that she's gone. I've spoken at funerals and written two obituaries, less than three years apart, for my mom and my sister. I wore the same dark blue dress to those two funerals. Four months after my sister's death, when I was packing up my clothes to move to a new home, I pulled that dress off its hanger. Pinned in place by a memory, I held the heavy material in my hands.

I splurged on that dress a few days before my mom was buried, not because I was feeling celebratory obviously, but because it felt like something I shouldn't do. When we found out she'd be going into hospice, I had rushed back to Texas from California with a wardrobe of jeans and pajamas. There was no way I was packing a funeral dress. That horrible thought did cross my mind as I threw clothes into my suitcase, but I just couldn't bring myself to do it.

Now we actually were burying my mom, so I was going to wear whatever the hell I wanted, except for the green Red Sox T-shirt I'd been cocooned in for eight days straight.

"What are you wearing?" is a fun question to ask if you're going to a birthday party or the Met Gala, but not so fun when you're dressing for your mother's funeral, which will be held outside on a cold, dreary Wednesday morning. After she died, my sisters and I asked each other what we were each wearing without a hint of joy. We may as well have been asking each other what we wanted our own tombstones to say.

"You can borrow something of mine," Kathryn offered, since she lived close by.

"No, that's okay," I said. "I'll just get something. I wish I could just wear a paper sack. I don't feel like dressing up at all."

"I don't either. It sounds horrible."

"Maybe we could all wear pink, since mom loved pale pink so much?" Amy offered.

Kathryn and I shot each other a stealth "No way in hell" look, but quickly found a way to say those words in a much nicer, gentler way.

"Um, Amy . . ."

"Okay, fine," Amy said.

"I am not in a pink mood at all," I said.

"Me, neither," Kathryn added.

"Neither am I, actually," Amy said. "I don't know what I was thinking. I just thought it would be sweet."

I needed something brand-new, something meant only for this occasion, only for my mom. I had no energy or desire to go out into the world and shop, so I went to the Nordstrom website and searched for dark blue dresses. My mom once told us that you don't *have* to wear black to funerals these days, and black just didn't seem right to me anyway. Neither did pink, purple, yellow, beige, brown, burnt umber, or turquoise. Dark blue was sorrowful and respectful, but not deeply depressing. After some lackluster scrolling, I found a knee-length, long-sleeved dress with pretty lace detail on the arms and torso. I would spend the $300 for this somber yet not completely depressing outfit, even though I'd probably never wear it again. I did wear it again, though, to Jackie's funeral less than three years later.

As I stood there, surrounded by moving boxes, weighing what to do with that dress, I noticed the black ribbon that was still pinned to the collar from Jackie's funeral. At some Jewish funerals, the immediate family members wear that torn black ribbon on their clothes as a sign of mourning. I unpinned the ribbon from the dress and put it into my bedside table drawer. Later that day I donated the dark blue dress to Goodwill. I was done. I wanted to show God or the Universe or whoever else was watching that by getting rid of that dress, I was closing the door to more grief. Before I dropped the dress off, I said a little prayer asking that the next owner wouldn't experience any grief, either. Maybe they could wear it to an upbeat cocktail party and reverse the cycle.

The unpredictable pathway through grief is fraught with these choices you don't want to make, like what to wear to a funeral. It's also full of "firsts" that may result in a condition I call Grief-Induced Emotional Avalanche (GIEA). My sister Jackie used to dye her dark brown hair bright red, and the first time I saw a stranger passing by with burgundy hair after Jackie died, I swear my heart stopped. GIEA is a close cousin of *heartsarnes*, but additional symptoms include dizziness, confusion, anger, deep sighs, and maybe a few tears.

I have yet to find a cure for GIEA, so I recommend supportive care, which may include taking a sick day to indulge in a good cry, online shopping for things you don't need but that bring you joy (overpriced scented candles work wonders for me), a *Bridgerton* binge, a fast run, or a long nap. Whatever you need to do to get through it (and you will get through it).

Over time, these episodes occur less frequently, but, at first, you just have to keep walking, not out or around, but through. William Faulkner wrote, "Between grief and nothing, I will take grief." It's a reminder that you're grieving because you've loved, and those land mines are there because that love stays with you, long after the person is gone. When you're standing right over a land mine, though, it's tough to find comfort in a quote.

One major first for me was when I went back to my job at an ad agency less than a week after my mom's funeral, mainly because I figured it would distract me and keep me from scrolling through old photos and crying all day. It was a solid plan, practical and wise. Focus on work, keep your head down, and go about your daily life.

That plan worked amazingly well for about half an hour. I tried so hard to pretend things were normal, and that I was just like all of my coworkers, bingeing on free La Croix and peanut butter-stuffed pretzels as if our lives depended on it, or at least as if the kitchen snacks could make up for what we dreamed our paychecks could be. But I wasn't like my coworkers. Not anymore.

After our morning meeting, which was my first meeting as a person who had lost a mom, I felt that uncontrollable surge of emotion and pain that anyone who has experienced

Potential "Firsts" That May Trigger GIEA

- Birthdays

- Mother's/Father's Day

- Anniversaries of any sort (proposal, wedding, first date, first vacation, first fight)

- First time you see someone with their same hair/walk/shoes/overall aura

- First Thanksgiving without them (any holiday, really)

- First time passing their favorite restaurant

- Sibling Day

- Love Your Pets Day

- Grandparents Day

- National Pizza Day (maybe they loved pizza)

great loss knows all too well. I snuck outside to calm myself down. As I walked quickly down the alleyway that separated our warehouse-like office from Ballona Creek, which is a Los Angeles waterway that is much less picturesque than it sounds, I got even more upset because I remembered that this was the walk I would take each workday when I called to check in on my mom during her nearly four years of chemo. Our conversations typically started like this:

"Hi, Mom, how're you feeling?"

"Shitty, honey. How're you?"

Laughing at the memory only made me cry harder. I couldn't call her anymore, ever. It was so final, but that impulse to call or text her lasts to this day, and I actually hope it never disappears. As sad as it is to grab your phone to call someone who is gone, it can also link you to them. For the briefest moment, they're still there. I know Amazon and Google and who knows what other companies are developing technologies that let you "talk" to the dead, but as much as I would love to talk to my mom about the latest Academy Awards fashion or ask my sister why she loved campy horror movies like *Nuke 'em High* so much, or why she dyed her hair burgundy all those years, I'll pass on that kind of phantom conversation. For now, at least.

As I walked down the alleyway behind the office on that sunny fall day, I calmed myself down once again. Eventually, I felt ready to head back inside and at least pretend to focus on work, or maybe just boost my paycheck by grabbing another coconut-flavored La Croix. As I was walking to the door, who comes out but the head of my department along with my immediate boss—a cooler-than-thou dude in a prog rock band called Annihilator. This was also a first. How do you pretend to keep it together the first time you bump into your bosses in the midst of an emotional break-down? In my case, the answer is: You don't.

So I lost it, again. I think this stage of grief could be called Hyperventilating because there is a very specific type of cry-ing that can occur during this time. It's the type where you cannot catch your breath, the waves are too strong to con-trol, and you find yourself, out of nowhere, doubled over and panic-sobbing in front of the people who have the power to hire and fire you.

My department head, the one who was not the drummer for Annihilator, hurried over to see if I was okay. Of course I was not okay, but that's what people do. They check.

"I think . . . I'm just . . ."

"It's okay," he said.

"I think I need to go home."

My first day back at work didn't last long, but at least I gave it a shot. I also got that "first" over with. After I'd gathered my laptop and purse and was driving out of the parking lot in my trusty Kia, who sauntered up to my car but the Annihilator himself. He was the last person I wanted to see, but I stopped and rolled down the window, because my mom raised me not to be a jerk. I was fully expecting him to remind me that a Kraken Rum write-up was due by end of day or to tell me that a Mountain Dew brief had come through and I needed to look at it ASAP and come back to him with fifteen bril-liant and bold ideas by the morning. Ideas that would shake up culture while also connecting with a diverse, multicultural audience (but not *too* diverse!) of impossibly cool and wealthy imaginary consumers.

"I'm sorry about your mom, dude," he said.

"Thank you."

I wasn't sure if I should get out of the car and hug him, or just sit there, like a stone.

"When my mom died, it was brutal," he said. "I quit my job and moved back to North Dakota to take care of her. It sucks, man. It's the hardest thing in the world to go through, so just take your time. I'm here if you need to talk or whatever."

I had no idea he had been through the loss of a parent. His declarations like, "I hate kids" and "Marriage is for assholes" never gave me the impression that he was a deeply empathetic human being, capable of true connection and love. His revelation, and his kind words, surprised me. I was pretty sure he hated me because I was a boring mom and not a twenty-three-year-old influencer with eight million TikTok followers, but this new development meant that maybe, possibly, we had something in common.

"I'm sorry you went through that," I said. "Thank you. That means a lot."

And it did.

We said goodbye, and as he walked off I drove away, east toward home, along the crowded Los Angeles freeways full of people whose lives and stories I would never know. Who had they lost? Were they having a normal day, or were they struggling through the motions, trapped inside a new reality, like me. I knew life was moving ahead, despite how I felt or who I had lost. It's a strange feeling, expecting the world to stop, take a pause, and sit in your pain with you. It doesn't stop, though. There is no pause, no shortcut back to where you were before.

After I left work that day, I picked Cole up early from day care, because there is nothing like an innocent little person to take your mind off your troubles and remind you that things might just be okay. Not easy or perfect, but okay. Steeling myself for the emotional aftershocks to come, I went back to work the next day, and each morning it got a little easier. I still cried next to Ballona Creek. I still stared, bleary-eyed, at my mom's old texts. I still hurt. My boss still demanded bold ideas that would shake the world. But each day, I went back. I got on that crowded freeway, and I drove.

Chapter 2
The Long Goodbye

The last thing you want to hear when you're doing a hospice orientation is a true crime story. I know this because one Sunday night in mid-November 2018, my sisters and I sat down at my parents' dining room table with a nurse named Glyn, who shared some *Texas Chainsaw Massacre*-esque family history with us. We were not there to hear about murder. We were there to learn how the next hours, days, or weeks would go as our mom left this world. No offense to Glyn, but regardless of whether she was talking about heaven or homicide, we were not thrilled to have her at the table. So when she abruptly jumped from explaining how to care for our mom at the end of her life (food, no; water, no; morphine, yes), to revealing her own familial horror story, our already raw, exposed nerves spontaneously caught fire and singed every molecule and atom in our immediate orbit. But subtly, with manners. God forbid we offend a guest.

It seems strange to find anything funny about the experience of hospice, but that's the only way I can process it or attempt to come close to explaining the absolute dread of

34

it all. By finding something, anything, humorous in those dark days. I guess I can thank Glyn for kicking things off.

Depending on what country you live in, what your insurance plan is (if you have insurance), and what kind of care you choose (if you have a choice), hospice is different for everyone. What is not different is that hospice is a time where someone is made comfortable as they die, whether they're at home or in some sort of facility. We wanted to bring our mom back to a cozy room that she so beautifully decorated herself, surrounded by familiar smells, sounds, lights, and antiques, without the beeping of machines or the roll of gurney wheels. Before Glyn came along, I thought hospice would be kind of like a movie. An Oscar-winning drama, not horror. It would be full of scenes where people hold hands and cry and say goodbye in a sad yet serene way. Candles would flicker and meaningful glances would be exchanged. Most importantly, a trained nurse would stand by twenty-four hours a day. I didn't think there would be benevolent, mandolin-playing cherubs floating around the room to guide us, but I did assume hospice would be less interactive. Basically, I thought we'd have more help.

At the dining room table that night with Glyn, I sat with Amy and Kathryn. Our dad tried to stay and listen to the instructions, but he was too distraught over losing the love of his life, the person he'd been with since Paschal High School, class of 1968. He left the table after about four minutes, which we understood. Our sister Jackie was in bad shape in New York, so she wasn't capable of helping. She knew that just as well as we did. We planned for her to fly out to Houston to say goodbye when we knew the very end was near, whatever day or week that might be. We didn't want it to be soon, but yet we did. What a horrible thing to feel. That's the ultimate cruelty of hospice. You don't want them to leave, but standing by and watching someone you love die, hour by hour, is an excruciating way to live.

Glyn sat at the head of the table and pulled a blue folder out of her bag. She fanned a few papers out in front of us and gently explained what we would need (morphine, mouth sponges, lavender oil for calming) and how we should behave (tell stories, say everything you need to say, be comforting). I had a pen and paper to take notes, as if I were sitting in a Classics class in college, listening to a lecture on *Antigone*, but unlike back then, I wasn't entirely confident about what I needed to write down. Do you write TELL STORIES, or should I just do that naturally? Does BE COMFORTING need to be put on my list, or is that obvious? Just in case, I wrote down whatever I could. Most end of life (EOL) advocates say you should have discussions with a loved one long before they enter hospice, and even before they experience any ailments, so that there is no confusion and you're not trying to make difficult decisions or figure out a Rubik's Cube of bureaucracy when you're in the throes of grief. Talking to a parent or loved one about these things while they're still healthy and (hopefully) years away from any health issues can make the conversations much easier to broach, since they're not weighted with fear and emotion.

Once someone is actually sick, these discussions are incredibly painful to bring up, especially with a loved one who has endured years of chemo treatments and has been fighting so hard to live. We were afraid to bring it up while our mom was still seeking out experimental procedures, because seeking treatment meant she had hope, and we could not bear to strip that away. We needed that hope, too. We were completely unprepared, so Glyn's orientation caught us off guard. I wrote down everything she said, to keep myself from having a panic attack.

"A nurse will come by once or twice a day for a few minutes to check your mother's vitals and make sure she's comfortable," Glyn said.

"You mean for a few hours, not minutes, right?" I asked.

"Not unless there's an emergency. And you can call us twenty-four hours a day."

"What's an emergency in hospice?"

"Well, if she seems overly anxious or panicked, for example. Otherwise the nurses come by to check and make sure she's comfortable."

This was my first clue that hospice was going to be nothing like the movies. It was going to be as real as you could possibly get, no filters, no cherubs, no round-the-clock help.

The hospice nurses aren't to blame for that. An analysis published in the medical journal *JAMA* in 2021 looked at 423 oncology outpatient encounters in the United States, and found that only 5 percent of those encounters included end-of-life discussions. Many oncologists glossed over topics like hospice care or end-of-life wishes, and included "optimistic future talk" to comfort patients, instead of sensitively helping them discuss the realities of their situation. My mother's oncologist was a saint, and he tried his best to give her hope. We all wanted to focus on that hope instead of on the harsh realities of her situation.

We should have enlisted a palliative care specialist much earlier to help us prepare for what was ahead, but, again, my mom was not ready to go, and we were not ready to open that door. Not until we absolutely had to, when her colon tore and the oncologist told us there was nothing anyone could do and it was now a matter of days or weeks, not six months or a year. By the time any real discussions happened, none of us were in our right minds. We were in a state of shock, signing papers, attempting to listen to nurses and doctors explain what happens next, but most of what they said did not reach us in any coherent way. So we signed the papers, we had the meetings, and we tried our best to understand and accept the fact that time was rushing ahead of us, decisions had to be made, and we just needed to hang on and try not to fall apart, for her and for each other.

I don't remember what prompted Glyn to segue from the topic of nursing visits to murder that first night. We *were* discussing death, so maybe she felt it was appropriate to let us know that we weren't the only ones hurting, and that some people had it much worse. Or maybe she was a sadistic caregiver who secretly strove to permanently scar the psyches of the bereaved to cover up her own long-ago trauma. Most likely, Glyn was hurting, too, and telling us her story was a form of connection. All I know is that what we actually needed at that time was for someone to heavily sedate us and put on *Home Alone*. We did not need more stress.

"I know this is hard," Glyn said softly.

What gave us away? The dark, fathomless pools of sorrow in our eyes? The fact that we each looked lost at sea, like dolphins who'd spent their entire lives in captivity, being hand-fed herring, only to suddenly find themselves released into a churning ocean at night?

"I don't usually share personal information, but did you hear about the Star murders?"

I did not write STAR MURDERS on my notepad. Instead, I stared at Glyn, this stranger with her tote bag and her pamphlets. My mom was lying twenty feet away from us. Murder was the absolute last thing I wanted to hear about.

Like three little well-mannered, shell-shocked robots, we told Glyn we had not heard about the Star murders.

"Well, it was in all the papers in Texas several years ago," she said. "My brother-in-law murdered my entire family up in Abilene, except for me and my husband, since we live in Houston. His last name was Star, so they called it the Star murders. It was awful. I just want you to know that I understand what you're going through, and you will get through this. Loss can be so very tough."

My sisters and I told Glyn how sorry we were and how horrible that sounded, but as I said these things I could feel my stress level rise, if that was even possible. I assumed it was already at its peak. Anxiety makes being uncomfortable feel dangerous, as if someone's words alone can send you into a type of purgatory, or even, somehow, kill you, pin you like a butterfly to a piece of foam, which is actually a completely barbaric practice that I will not go into, because it might actually give you anxiety. As far as stress levels go, Glyn's story cranked the gears. What I didn't realize at the time was that the entire hospice experience would continue on that trajectory. I went on to carry that anxiety with me for nearly a year, which was a fact I would only discover many months later, when I finally sought help.

As disturbing as Glyn's orientation was, she was right. Loss can be so very tough. I would imagine anyone who goes into hospice care is giving, nurturing, and kind, because it cannot be an easy job. Once we accepted the fact that this was going to be much harder on us than we ever expected, my sisters and I banded together. We divided up the things that needed to be taken care of, and turned into a crack team of caregivers. Amy and I handled the morphine, and Kathryn handled . . . everything else. Phone calls and papers that needed signing. Scheduling medication drop-offs and regulating visitors so we didn't get overwhelmed. We could have crumbled under the pressure, but that didn't feel like an option. The least we could do for the woman who gave birth to us, changed our diapers, comforted us in heartbreak, and taught us to always wear a little lipstick was to take care of her in her final days.

Kathryn lived about twenty minutes away from our parents and she had three young kids to wrangle, which is why Amy and I administered the oral morphine every two hours. We were staying at the house and our entire existence could revolve around those two-hour blocks of time. Neither of us would be described as mind-blowingly thorough and organized (that is Kathryn's strength), so the handwritten chart we devised to keep track of when we'd last given our mom the drug that would keep her from feeling pain looked like the cryptic scribblings of two sleep-deprived lunatics who were in way over their heads. It did the job, though. We put every ounce of energy in our reserves into scribbling down the exact timing of those two-hour morphine doses, because the thought of missing one, or even being five minutes late to give one, meant that our mom might feel pain. Because of the pressure and the horrible responsibility of this, we quickly became walking zombies. I remember, a few days in, contemplating going on a run just to step outside into fresh air. I imagined myself attempting to jog, and in my mind it was like trudging through wet cement. There was no way I could move my limbs with any vigor at all. In some moments, it took everything I had to just stand up off the couch and get some water. Even with a whole hospice "team" assigned to our case, it felt like we were on our own, as if someone said, "Hey, during the most psychologically and emotionally agonizing days of your life, we're going to trust you to measure medications and make sure your mom dies peacefully, even though you have zero training and you're absolutely terrified that you're going to do something wrong, something that will haunt you the rest of your life. But anyway, good luck!" No one told us to take care of ourselves, to step outside and take a walk. Even if they had, it wouldn't have changed the fact that we very quickly became a house full of hollow-eyed automatons, trudging from room to room and mumbling things like:

"Did you figure out mom's insurance today?"

"What time did they say the hospice nurse was coming?"

"What day should we have the funeral director come?"

"What day is it anyway?"

"Who do we call to order more morphine?"

"The hospital called. They said we forgot to sign a form."

"The funeral director said he wants to talk to someone at the hospice place, but they're not calling him back."

Somehow, calls were made and emails were sent, even though we could barely remember what month it was, whether or not we'd brushed our teeth that morning, or when the last time we showered was.

"Bereavement care in America is broken, if it even exists," says Joyal Mulheron, founder of Evermore, a nonprofit focused on improving the lives of bereaved families through research, policy, and education. Mulheron, a public policy expert who has worked with Michelle Obama's Partnership for a Healthier America, lost her infant daughter Eleanora over ten years ago. She saw firsthand how "broken" the system was when insurance companies would call her during her daughter's pediatric in-home hospice, and ask how many days or weeks it would be until her daughter passed away. Mulheron said she had twenty-three providers, but she was the one doing the caloric calculations, making sure her daughter was getting enough nutrition to keep her comfortable. Mulheron wasn't sleeping, because how could she? During that time, the company she worked for asked for her resignation, since she was caring for her daughter and couldn't devote herself to the job as she once had. Now, she's working to change those systems that were so broken for her, and for so many others.

"No one in America is squarely looking at bereavement policy, so it becomes a hodgepodge," she says. "There is a collective sense that the system isn't well tuned to attend to people."

It's not that the nurses who came by during my mom's hospice weren't caring. It's just that they popped in and out, and it was all so much more clinical and morbid than I ever expected it to be. I know it's *death*, but I guess I expected some sort of metaphorical or actual protective screen between myself and what was happening to my mom. In hospice, there is no screen—real or imaginary. If you're not a nurse, paramedic, forensic examiner, soldier, war photographer, serial killer, or ER doctor, you're likely not used to witnessing the end of life. The nurses were kind, but also honest, and by *honest* I mean they had to explain things that, to us, were pretty upsetting. We were told about "agitated delirium," which we saw during our mom's last days in the hospital, when she was hallucinating children in the corner, or hurling a fidget apron across the room. The nurses gave her the apron, which is often used by dementia patients to help with sensory stimulation, to keep her hands busy, but it only upped her agitation level. I understood her need to fling away that colorful apron, festooned with buttons and Velcro and zippers that were meant to distract her, or soothe her, or both. It looked like something a Holly Hobbie rag doll or a Cottagecore influencer would wear. As delirious as she was, she knew she was dying. My mom was pissed. She wasn't a child. She didn't want to play with Velcro. She wanted her fucking life back. She had every right to be angry, and so did we. It wasn't the fault of the oncologists, or the nurses, GI specialists, internists, or social workers. It wasn't the fault of the rabbi who came to visit in the hospital, freaking us out with the finality of his presence. There was no one to blame, no one to curse, except the universe maybe, or fate. Which really means, there is no place to successfully hurl your sorrow or frustration when someone you love is dying, or if you're the one dying. So you lob an apron full of zippers across the room.

As the days dragged on, the hospice nurses explained the signs of death we might see, like mottling, when her skin would begin to look like marble, streaked by red and purple hues I hope never to see again, but that I likely will. As someone whose blood pressure plummets whenever I have a small vial of blood drawn, these were horrible things to learn about, and to hear. As hard as it was, I know it was their job to prepare us. It probably would have been worse if they hadn't. By the last few days, though, I got to the point where if I heard one more hospice nurse say, "I predict it won't be more than forty-eight hours. Seen any mottling today?" I was going to, like Glyn's brother-in-law, turn murderous.

After the first sleepless night of trying to do it all our-selves, my dad decided to pay for a nurse to come from ten at night until five in the morning; otherwise, I'm not sure we could have held it together. The night nurse's name was, of all things, Angel, and she lived up to that name. She was gentle and empathetic. She held our mom's hand and gave us much-needed hugs. At that time I didn't know you could hire death doulas to come help you through the process, so Angel was all we had. The hospice care did send a chaplain over one day. We'd spoken to a rabbi, and we were planning a Jewish funeral, which meant that we would each have to step up and toss a shovelful of dirt onto the casket. It's a tradition that's deeply emotional, and also therapeutic, since you're forced to do something so mundane, so *real*. We didn't talk to the chaplain about any of that, though. We just told him we were hurting, and that we appreciated him coming to the house and sitting with us. He didn't stay long, but he told us he'd come back any time. I'll likely never see that chaplain again. I don't remember his name or what he wore, but I do know he gave us comfort at a time when the smallest gesture of kindness felt monumental.

Tony Pham has dedicated his career to those gestures of kindness. He's a certified death doula and meditation instructor, based in New York. He provides spiritual companionship to both the person dying and the grieving family. He was drawn to the profession after losing both of his maternal grandparents in quick succession. That led him to start having those uncomfortable talks with his parents about wills and end-of-life wishes early on. His parents resisted at first, but eventually they came around and were even appreciative that he'd brought it up. As tough as it may be at times, he says his work with grieving families has been a "humbling and moving experience. Learning to grieve becomes an essential part of being human. If we bottle it up, we're not giving ourselves the full experience of what it is to be alive."

When I told Pham about my own hospice experience, and about how clinical so much of it felt, he wasn't surprised. Part of the reason he went into this kind of work was to help it feel less clinical, and more humane. He often works with families who already have a hospice team assigned, just as a birth doula might be there for a delivery in the hospital, even though they're not part of the "official" team.

"I consider both birth and death to be passageways and significant moments of transition. It is just that much of Western society has chosen to normalize anticipating birth while resisting death," Pham says. "How does one prepare for what is ultimately a mystery? I try to encourage people to take time to start reflecting, and to compassionately accompany people through the fear."

Pham often helps the person who is dying, but the friends and family sitting by their side need that support, too. I feared for my mom, although I knew she was not in great pain, thanks to the barely legible chart Amy and I lived by. During orientation, Glyn told us that hospice patients often go through a "life review," where they start reflecting on all their memories and milestones, from childhood to the present, before they pass away. It's a lovely thought, that they're revisiting all the moments, good and bad, before they can leave. My mom wasn't speaking or opening her eyes, but we knew she could hear us, and so we said everything we needed and wanted to say, and then some. We are a very affectionate and expressive family. My sisters and I probably say "I love you" four or five times at the end of each phone call, so our mom got an earful in her final days. We talked so much that maybe she was ready to go, just so we'd shut up.

"I encourage people to do retrospective things, like talk about regrets or things they are proud of or appreciate," Pham says. "That part of the process is so important." He also encourages family and friends to find a ritual that might help them cope with their emotions. He says often, that ritual depends on the culture of the grieving. Maybe it's something like the washing of hands and feet before a prayer, or everyone standing in a circle holding hands in silence. The key is that the ritual has to feel authentic, and not forced. "All of these things help as far as catharsis," Pham says. "I let people come to it themselves."

Our ritual, if you can call it that, was sitting as close to my mom as possible, for much of the day. It was holding her hand and telling stories. It was gently placing dots of lavender oil on her temples, hoping it would calm her, and us.

As traumatic as our eight days of hospice were, we got to sit with our mom, every minute if we wanted to. We got to give her hugs and kiss her forehead. We got to tell stories and laugh about things we remembered, which is a privilege that was taken from anyone who lost a loved one during the early days of the pandemic. I thought of them often, during those uncertain, heartbreaking months of early 2020. Strangers I read about in articles or heard about on the news, saying good-bye via FaceTime. Friends of friends, someone on Twitter I'd never met but who was sharing their most personal sorrows via an app. I used to think I would never wish hospice on anyone, until I imagined what it would be like not to have had it at all.

A 2017 study conducted by the Kaiser Family Foundation (KFF) and *The Economist* asked a random selection of over four thousand adults eighteen years and older in the United States, Brazil, Japan, and Italy about their opinions of hospice care. They found that among the 70 percent of participants who said they knew at least a little bit about hospice care, only 9 percent said they had a negative opinion of hospice. That doesn't mean that each of them had actu-ally experienced hospice, and Liz Hamel, vice president and director of public opinion and survey research at KFF, says of hospice care in the United States, "There is a fair amount of confusion, and people's wishes are not necessarily matching up with what happens. There is a mismatch in expectations versus reality." Hamel says people need to understand how much they may be asked to do to help a loved one during hospice, and they need to advocate for themselves.

"It's harder than people think it's going to be and people are not prepared," Hamel says. "The amount that people have to pay in the United States is also an added stress that's not there in other countries."

Another issue is that, as a society, we're often led to believe that if we truly love a person, we'll bring them home to die. Choosing to stay in the hospital or in a hospice care facility can make family members feel guilty, as if they're not doing enough. Dr. Melissa Wachterman, a palliative care physician at Harvard Medical School, wrote an article published in the *New England Journal of Medicine*, titled "Where Americans Die—Is There Really No Place Like Home?" Wachterman has witnessed how patients and families handle EOL decisions over the course of more than fifteen years, and she believes, like Joyal Mulheron, that policy changes and attitudes surrounding bereavement care need to change.

"Some people have this vision that hospice is going to take care of everything, and they don't," Wachterman says. "I feel strongly that a large burden is placed on families when loved ones die at home." That's not to say that Wachterman believes everyone should die in a hospital, but she thinks that families should be educated early on about what home hospice entails, and they should be freed from the societal pressure that says if you love someone, you bring them home to die.

"I don't want to throw hospice under the bus," Wachterman says. "There are hospices that offer more and do it really great. As a society we can do better by seriously ill patients, and palliative care is just a piece of that. We need to increase support for home death."

When Wachterman talks to patients about tough topics, like where they want to die, she phrases it in a way that I love, and that I wish I'd known when my mom was still alive. She tells them, "We're going to go somewhere scary for a moment, but you're not there yet. We're going to open this box and peek inside, and then we can close the box."

Maybe that would have helped us all if we'd had those types of conversations early on, since framing it that way feels less bleak. Instead, we felt like we were totally on our own.

You can't force a nurse to stay around the clock if your insurance doesn't cover it and the cost is prohibitive, but you can make calls, ask for more help, tell them you're not sure you can take another day of this existence and can someone please just stop by one more time. My sisters and I didn't know we had it in us, the ability to help our own mom die peacefully. We had our moments of guilt, of course. Amy and I would look at each other as we administered the oral morphine yet again, and say, "Are we killing her? Is this horrible? What are we doing?" Intellectually, we understood that there was nothing a doctor or nurse or death doula could do to save our mom, and that giving her morphine was a gesture of ultimate love, but still. What a thing to have to do. It still haunts us to this day.

Amy and I kept the morphine up in a kitchen cabinet, away from the curious, searching hands of my nephew, who was five at the time. Our two-hour routine went like this: Take out the medication, administer the dose, put it back in the cabinet, wait two hours, repeat. Since time was a melting Salvador Dalí clock to us, I don't know what day or hour it was when we went to retrieve the vial and discovered that it wasn't in its usual spot. I do clearly remember the panic and fear I experienced, not being able to find that medication that was the only thing keeping my mom from feeling pain. We rushed around, looking under couches and behind pillows, in drawers and purses and corners. We called about getting more medication, but it wouldn't come soon enough. We placed the order anyway. My only clue that this panic happened in the evening was that our search led Amy and me outside, to a large trash can, where, without gloves, we started frantically picking through old garbage bags. The porch light allowed us to see in the dark as we scavenged through old coffee grinds, wadded up napkins, and rotted apple cores, looking for that small vial.

By some miracle, Amy and I didn't get angry at each other. We didn't allow our frustration and fear to turn to blame, because both of us were capable of losing the medication. We searched, together, without anger. The anger would come soon enough, but, at that moment, we were united in our mission. We would not stop until we found the morphine. We were sure that we would soon reach into one of those bags and triumphantly pull out the little vial, holding it up to the semi-starry sky before dashing back inside to give it to our mom. Instead, in the midst of our search, our family friends Doug and Sally walked up, clearly startled by the sight of us looking so distraught, surrounded by trash. We forgot they were coming to say goodbye to our mom, and their presence and the pity on their faces ended our frenzy. It was time to go back inside and regroup, which meant go back inside and continue to ransack the house until we found the vial of morphine or the new morphine was dropped off, whenever that might be.

We walked into the house, and there it was, right there on the table by our mom's hospice bed, next to the lavender oil. How had we missed it? Why did we spend minutes that felt like hours looking for this thing? We immediately gave it to our mom and put it back in the cabinet. It didn't matter who left it there. All that mattered was that it was found.

My sisters and I were united in our mission the majority of the time, but intense stress can turn even the most harmonious relationships into a *Real Housewives* battle royale situation. The morning after our morphine scare, Amy and I did, finally, snap. I know it was morning because I ended up running down a busy street in Houston just after sunrise, barefoot and in my pajamas.

I have no idea what caused us to start fighting. In high school, if Amy wore too much perfume I would lose my mind because I drove her to school, and the smell was so strong in the car that I'd feel sick. Maybe I was being a tiny bit melodramatic, but she did douse herself. I would also become enraged if she took my hairbrush or lied and said she didn't have my vintage brown velvet vest (it was the 1990s and it was adorable, I swear), even though I'd just found it in her closet underneath my beloved white linen overalls. When these arguments happened back then, we'd be at each other's throats for the entire six-minute drive to high school, until we'd inevitably forgive each other and hug it out in the parking lot while saying "I love you" sixteen times before heading into class.

The morning of our hospice fight, I remember storming out of the house and yelling, "When is the last time YOU took a 5 a.m. shift!"

Whoops.

That led to Amy chasing behind me and screaming: "*EXCUSE ME*??!!!!"

That's not all she said. There was more. So much more.

As she screamed, I rage-walked down the driveway, out the gate, and along the sidewalk in my ratty pajamas that hadn't been washed in a week. I had no destination, no phone, no shoes, no bra, no pride. I just needed out. I needed to allow myself to get pissed off and lose it for a minute. You don't need to consult a professional to figure out why I needed to storm off, or why my sister needed to scream. We all needed to rage. I rushed past people walking their labradoodles and pugs, eventually realizing how I must have looked to them: like a disheveled woman on a rage walk. Eventually, my pace slowed, and I felt awful. Almost as quickly as I stormed off, I hurried back to hug it out and apologize and tell Amy forty-five times how much I loved her and that I couldn't do any of this without her. We hugged as if our lives depended on it, just as we had back in high school. When we parted, we remained united in our mission: to survive that horrible time, to help our mom, to make it through another day.

Families can be torn apart by inheritances or divorce or petty grievances. Siblings sometimes become estranged for decades. Cousins turn into enemies, and aunts and uncles can feel like strangers. These separations can be healthy, if the relationship is toxic or harmful. For us, in hospice, and in death, we became even closer, minus the one moment of Bravo-esque drama. I'm not sure if having round-the-clock help would have made things less intense. It would have helped a little bit, but as traumatic as that hospice experience was, I remember my sisters always there by my side. I remember the friends and neighbors who stopped by for a minute or an hour. The kind words and the meals. I remember my cousin Courtney driving almost five hours to stay one night and help. I remember making the call to Jerett to tell him it was time for him to fly out to Houston from Los Angeles with Cole, who was only thirteen months old. When he told me he'd buy a ticket for the following day, I experienced a fear I'd never imagined I would have.

I was terrified that I would have no love or energy at all to give to my son. That fear was frighteningly real. I didn't know if I could take care of my mom, go through losing her, and also be a mother to my own child. I was convinced I would fail him. How do we handle anything other than our grief when we're in the depths of it? How do we manage work and childcare and relationships, when we have so much heaviness pulling us to the ground? In the toughest moments, it's hard to imagine giving one more ounce of yourself away. I had very little confidence that I could take on anything other than administering medications and keeping myself awake, and that scared me. What if I couldn't even look at my son, or hold him, when I saw him again? What if he needed me and I just wasn't capable of comforting him? I could not imagine enduring that week with a baby to care for, and I know that so many caregivers have no choice in this. They have to work and watch their children and also care for a sick or dying parent or spouse. I got to take off work and my husband had our son, so in many ways I had it easy. And if what I had was easy compared to others, it's a miracle that anyone can handle hospice, or caregiving, at all.

"When a loved one is transitioning, there's a natural human tendency to go into self-sacrifice mode," Pham says.

Part of his job is to remind people that taking care of yourself is just as important as taking care of your loved one. Pham listens to people's needs, helps them manage visitors, and allows them to take breaks without feeling guilt, so they don't run themselves into the ground. Not everyone can have a doula by their side during hospice, but it's good advice, hard as it may be to actually follow through with it.

When Jerett walked into the house that Thursday with Cole, to my relief I hurried over to them and felt a rush of love. There was more to give, and what I hadn't realized was that my son would restore my energy, instead of sucking me dry. My mom was slowly leaving, but I had this child to feed and change and medicate since, in keeping with Murphy's Law of Parenting, my kid happened to get a virus right at that time. He had a high fever and was more lethargic than I'd ever seen him. Thankfully, I wanted to hold him and help him, not turn him away.

For the next few days, the hours melted away, and we went through the motions of living, existing within a space that felt suspended just outside the limits of everyday life. The hospice nurses continued to say, "I don't think it'll be more than twenty-four hours," and we continued to tell my mom how much we loved her, how lucky we were to have had her. We defrosted lasagnas and casseroles and barely ate them. We drank wine, without joy. By the last two days, which we did not know at the time would be the last two days, we finally found the courage to say, "Mom, it's okay now. You can go."

Jackie flew in from New York that Saturday to say goodbye. She looked fragile and lost in her addiction. She came with Niall and her incredible best friend Amelia, who was several years sober and who promised us she would get Jackie to Houston and then back to New York safely. My dad asked Jackie to tell our mom that she would get sober for her, and as Jackie said her goodbyes, she repeated the words she was asked to say. You can't force an alcoholic to make those promises, though. I wish overcoming an addiction were that simple. Despite the promise she whispered, Jackie didn't get sober for a long time. Eventually she did, for nearly a year, but not that night, or the next.

After about an hour, Jackie said goodbye, hugged our mom, and left. As she walked away, down the driveway and toward the dark street to the car, I had no way of knowing that would be the last time I would see my sister alive. If I'd known, I would have held her tighter. I wouldn't have let her go.

Hospice can make you believe in things you might normally dismiss. For example, I think our mom was waiting to pass away until she could see Jackie one more time. These odd occurrences become much more than pretty tales we tell ourselves—that someone is holding on to see a loved one before they die, or that a soul leaves a body. After going through it, I do believe these things are real. I need to believe it.

The next morning, the Sunday after Thanksgiving, the house was quiet and calm. We were sitting in the den, a room away from my mom, talking and watching who knows what on TV. We were more melancholy than usual, I think because seeing Jackie in that state was hard. For so many years, it often felt as if there were a missing cutout of our sister, during holidays or birthdays or weekend family trips. Loving an addict means living with that empty space much of the time. She was in that room with us that morning, but not, and we missed her—the Jackie we knew, the one who would have been right there at our mom's side every moment, if the alcohol wasn't in control. If you haven't lived with an addict or alcoholic in your life, it might seem callous on our part that my sister couldn't or didn't stay, but the depths of complexity that go along with these relationships become an impossible tangle of guilt and anger, compassion, anxiety, frustration, and pain. Above all, we loved her. That didn't mean we could handle her at her worst, especially at a time when we could barely handle ourselves.

Eventually, without saying anything, my dad got up to check on my mom. After a few minutes, he walked back into the room.

"Girls?" he said, looking at the floor. He has a way of sighing, one shoulder slumped lower than the other, that telegraphs his pain. He didn't have to say anything else. We knew that she was gone.

It's common for hospice nurses to tell family or friends that it's important to leave the dying person alone from time to time. Even if they're not responsive, they may feel afraid to die in front of a spouse or child or grandchild, so giving them that space to leave can be important. The night before my mom died, my brother-in-law Mike took my young niece and nephew back home, about four hours north of Houston to Fort Worth. The house was peaceful that next morning. The grandkids weren't there to witness what happened next, and I will always believe she not only waited for Jackie to come say goodbye, but that she needed her grandchildren to leave, to not have a memory of her dying, before she could go. Her empathy was never ending, even at her moment of death.

And so, together that morning, we walked into the room to be with her one final time. Those moments are a blur to me now. What was said, how our bodies moved through space. It's an impression, vague and yet full of sorrow. There is no way, for me at least, to process or analyze the actual moment you realize a mother, your mother, has left. What is your life going to be like without the person who raised you? What does it mean that she's gone—your touchstone, the one who, even as she drove you nuts, always made you feel most like yourself? *No one knows you like your mother*, people often say. So how do you continue without this person, who was so much a part of you? The person who gave you your laugh, your sense of humor, your love of Natalie Wood's movies and Toni Morrison's writing. That shift in existence is a shimmer, imperceptible, unmooring. Maybe that's why, looking back, all I can ever remember in that room is the sunlight, and silence.

Eventually, we had to call the hospice nurses and Lev the funeral director. Little did we know he would come back into our lives two and a half years later, sooner than we would have liked, leading us to call him Uncle Lev. We had to let them know our mom had died, so they could make arrangements. As devastated as we were, we made sure to tell Lev that he'd better bury our mom with her wig on, or else. A Texas belle to the end, she hated losing her hair, and she would not just haunt us but kill us in our sleep if we let Lev bury her without that wig. It sounds ridiculous, but it was important to us, because we knew it would have been important to her. Lev, having no doubt heard his share of strange burial requests over the years, completely understood. After we spoke to him, we also needed to safely dispose of the morphine, tell other family members, and give our own kids the million things they needed from us. We were compelled to move forward, whether we liked it or not.

There's a tradition in Judaism where, after sitting shiva, which is the weeklong mourning period, the family goes outside and walks around the block together. It signifies the bereaved reentering society. It's supposed to happen a week after the burial, but we're not exactly traditional, so the morning my mom died, when they came to take her away, my dad said he wanted us all to go outside and walk around the block, in keeping with that tradition, sort of. It was a gorgeous day, the kind of sunny, temperate weather our mom loved. Santa Barbara weather, she would have said. She couldn't stand the muggy Houston summers. She was a Texan to her core, though, so despite her love of places like Santa Barbara, she never would have lived anywhere else. Over the years, whenever I called her during the month of August and asked how she was, she would inevitably say, "Well, it's hotter than nine kinds of hell, honey. How're you?" In a way it's oddly comforting knowing that the day she left, it was her ideal kind of day.

We stepped outside. I held Cole in my arms, and, together, we walked—my dad, Amy, Kathryn, my brother-in-law Ben, Jerett, and my one-year-old niece Sutton. Rows of old live oak trees canopied the streets. Those oaks are what I love most about Houston. They're the prettiest things in the city, as far as I'm concerned. Historic, majestic, and, maybe most appealing in a metropolis that often hits "nine kinds of hell" triple-digit temperatures, shady. I'm not sure what anyone said during our walk, if we said much of anything at all. I think we were mostly silent. It takes much longer than a simple stroll for loss to settle in, if it settles at all. It's still settling around me, years after that walk below the oaks.

That Sunday afternoon, we wound through streets where kids played football and neighbors watered lawns. Maybe to them we just looked like an exceptionally pensive family taking a stroll, but that walk, which lasted much longer than a few blocks, wasn't symbolic of us reentering society. It was us actually, physically entering a new existence. Moving into a world where we would carry grief with us, always. None of us knew what was ahead, or how we would cope or function. We did know that millions of people had experienced grief of this depth, every day, for centuries, and somehow they endured. And so, beneath the shady oaks, we walked, away from that horrible hospice week and into the rest of our lives, without her.

Chapter 3
Chicken Soup, Gumbo, and a Bucket of KFC

In ancient Egypt, food offerings were often left in tombs. Royals tended to get things like veal while the regular folks got off-brand mutton—go figure. In parts of Thailand, friends and relatives never bring noodle dishes to the bereaved, because they symbolize ropes that could bind the deceased's soul to their former life and prevent them from moving on. Fiambre is a Guatemalan salad with up to fifty ingredients that's served during Day of the Dead and during bereavement. And in Houston, Texas, in the fall of 2018, Original Recipe Kentucky Fried Chicken unofficially entered the pantheon of foods that sustain and uplift people in mourning.

In the days following my mom's death, a variation of "Stick it in the freezer and pop it in the oven whenever you want!" appeared via text throughout the day. My messages ping-ponged between "Are you okay?" and "I sent baked ziti. Stick it in the freezer and pop it in the oven whenever you want." Within twenty-four hours, my dad's refrigerator and freezer shelves were crammed with homemade gumbo and meatballs and chicken soup, sent by friends and neighbors. We also got gigantic salads (none with fifty ingredients, but they were big enough), platters of brownies, green bean casseroles, bagels and lox, fruit platters, sandwich trays, enchilada casseroles, and pizza. Things stacked up so quickly, it took us ten minutes of stress and toil just to pull a jar of pickles out of the refrigerator without creating an avalanche of marinara sauce and queso. As perilous as pulling out a snack became, this arsenal of wholesome(ish) comfort food freed us from cooking or expending energy we didn't have to put toward a daunting task like deciding what to eat. This is what so many of us around the world do when faced with hardship. We feed each other dishes that are easy to heat up and that can last for days or weeks. And in the American South, the more butter those dishes are made with, the better.

Good food is everything that grief is not: celebratory, exciting, life-affirming, joyous. In the early days of grief, I could barely stomach a piece of plain toast, much less some lasagna or a large fajita platter. At some point during the long, oppressive days spent at my mom's hospital bedside right before we brought her home for hospice, I remember being sent down to the cafeteria by my dad to take a break and get some food. It was the last thing I wanted, but breaks are necessary when you're sitting, waiting, listening to the beep of medical equipment and the roll of gurney wheels out in the hallway for hours on end. What you're waiting for is something unimaginable. You're stuck inside a place and time you never asked for, with no escape. There is only one ending to the story you've found yourself in, and you're heading to that conclusion whether you like it or not. You cannot claw or cry or beg your way out. It's the most tortuous kind of waiting, watching someone you love die. But all you can do is wait. And, I guess, eat. Or try to.

I reluctantly followed my dad's advice that day in the hospital and went looking for the cafeteria. It was something to do, somewhere to go, to break up the bouts of staring up at figure skating on the hospital room television or scrolling celebrity Instagram in search of something pretty and colorful that might give me a desperately needed boost of serotonin.

I took the elevator to the lobby, followed the signs to the cafeteria, and wandered in, grabbing a pale blue plastic tray as I entered. As far as dining choices go, you cannot get much bleaker than a hospital cafeteria. Maybe prison is worse? A rundown flea market in Reno? Actual hell? I glanced at the faces of the strangers pretending to nibble flimsy ham sandwiches and shellacked mashed potatoes, people who were most likely not having their best day, or their best lunch. Even the doctors and nurses and staff would probably rather be anywhere else. People trudged through buffet lines and slouched over untouched trays of food, trying their best to feed themselves as if life were going on as it always had, as if this were just another meal.

I walked past the mashed potatoes, the meat loaf, and the cauldrons of gloppy soup, feeling queasy. The only thing that wound up on my plate was a pile of wilty, blanched green beans that looked as pathetic as I felt. The thought of anything with sauce or flavor or richness turned my stomach, and the beans were the most feeble and flavorless thing I could find. They fit my mental and emotional state perfectly. Despite our cosmic link, looking down at the sad pile on my tray triggered something in me. It was all so awful. The quiet, drab cafeteria with orange and brown paper turkeys decorating the walls for Thanksgiving. The jaundiced glare of fluorescent lights. The disgusting green beans that looked like the very life had been sucked right out of them. And, of course, my mom, upstairs in that small room, barely speaking, unable to eat because of the tear in her colon, only waking to hallucinate a little boy in the corner of the room or, if I was lucky, to remember that I was her eldest daughter, take my hand, and call me by my name.

Before I even paid for the green beans, I called Jerett, who was back in California at work. I needed to do something to steady myself so I didn't wind up weeping, dejected, and covered in soggy green beans on the cafeteria floor.

"Are you okay?" he answered.

"No. I'm not. I can't even look at my green beans."

"What's wrong with them?"

"They're just . . . so sad."

"Can you get a sandwich instead?"

"A sandwich won't help."

"Soup?"

"It's cream of mushroom! It's not about the soup. I'm not even hungry."

"Take some deep breaths. You're going to be okay."

"This is the worst feeling in the world. It hurts too much."

I didn't fall to the floor, but I did weep, loud and hard, right there next to the cashier. Judging by her non-reaction, I'm sure she'd witnessed a similar scene many times before. I tried to express to Jerett what I was feeling, but how do you explain grief, in its most piercing moments? Terrible, painful, torturous? Nothing captures the fathoms of conflicting emotions, the desire to punch holes through walls or scream or just disappear. The impulse to give up, and the will to take a deep breath followed by the resolve to keep going. That stubborn drive to keep it together, when all you want to do is fall apart or, better yet, fade away, back into the past.

I couldn't find the words to explain my grief, so I projected everything onto those stupid green beans, which I'm sure led to Jerett feeling extremely confused as to why an edible seed pod was so triggering for me. I eventually pulled it together, said goodbye, paid up, and managed to eat a few bites. The green beans tasted like wet cardboard dusted with a single grain of salt. The flavor (or lack of flavor) didn't lift my mood or give me hope, but it did give me the strength to go back upstairs, face a reality I did not want, hold my mom's hand, and wait.

A little over a week later, when my mom was home for hospice, I sat on a small white couch with Amy. The couch was in a sitting room at my parents' house, about a foot away from the bed that the hospice team had wheeled in for my mom to spend her last days and nights. I don't know what Amy and I talked about on that couch at that moment. We could have been sharing funny memories of our mom, or talking about the movies she introduced us to, like *Splendor in the Grass* or *Hud*. Maybe we talked about her "famous" recipes, and the foods we'd miss—her pumpkin trifle dessert, homemade chicken soup, skillet fried chicken ("Girls, if you make fried chicken without buttermilk, it's not worth eating"), and tomato pie. Most likely, though, we were talking about how tired we both were, how we wanted this to all be over, but then again we didn't, because that would mean only one thing. We weren't expecting anyone to come by, so when the doorbell rang we forced ourselves up off the couch to see who it was.

I hadn't seen Meredith, or Mrs. Griffis as I called her as a child, in years. I had practically grown up at her house, which was around the corner from my own, playing or spending the night with her daughter, my best friend, Liza. I especially loved being at Liza's house during the Christmas holidays. We made gingerbread houses by sticking graham crackers to the outside of milk cartons using icing as "glue." Being one of the lone Jewish kids in the neighborhood who didn't have Christmas décor or holiday lights, their massive, sparkly tree rocked my world. And Meredith's food. Oh, the food. Home-made fudge, chocolate pecan pie, lemon bars, and beef brisket. Between the tinsel, the wooden Nutcracker soldiers, and the sugar cookies, it was a magical place for a kid to hang out.

Meredith and my mom became close, but in the last ten or fifteen years of her life my mom had closed herself off from many of the friends she once knew and loved. My sister's alcoholism caused my mom to withdraw, and she found it hard to be as lively and social as she had once been. If she had only opened up about it, I'm sure most of her friends would have understood. I think she felt such a stigma, though, and such pain, that she chose to retreat. Like many parents of alcoholics or addicts, my mother blamed herself. Did this happen to Jackie because my mom had such a difficult labor with her? Was it because she didn't understand Jackie's learn-ing differences early enough? Did she fail her in some other way? These are all reasons my mom would give for Jackie's disease. Eventually, thanks to group therapy, she came to semi-understand that it wasn't her fault, but not completely. Because of this guilt, she canceled lunch plans and screened calls. She pulled away. Still, despite the years of distance, there was Meredith, Mrs. Griffis, standing at our door, holding a large bucket of Kentucky Fried Chicken.

A bucket of KFC might not sound like an odd thing to bring to a grieving family, but my memories of Mrs. Griffis involved fine china, homemade fudge, liver pâtés, and heirloom snow sled ornaments. She was braised quail and champagne, not Original Recipe chicken and Dr Pepper. But I guess I'd been wrong all those years. Or maybe she lightly dusted her KFC with rare truffle oil and served it on a bed of Belgian endive and chervil leaves.

Amy and I opened the door, forcing ourselves to find the energy to at least semi-smile and invite her in. Old Southern manners die hard or, more accurately, they never die because you were raised to be polite, no matter how godawful you felt. "Kill them with kindness" was about as mean as I was raised to be. "Don't be a Hateful Hannah" was a phrase that was drilled into us growing up, so, yes, we were gearing up to invite Meredith in and offer her some iced tea. The bucket of chicken was thoughtful, but the kindest gesture was Meredith handing us the food and then immediately saying, "You don't need to invite me in. I just wanted to bring this by. I love you and I'm here if you need anything at all."

And then, without waiting for us to answer, she hurried off. It was the most compassionate thing she could have done, letting us be, not forcing us to interact or expend any more energy offering her a drink or engaging in small talk.

The lack of expectations, the simplicity of it all, was such a relief. Sometimes there is just not much you can say, so you say it with food, without expecting anything in return.

As soon as we closed the door, Amy and I took that bucket of KFC into the kitchen, pulled off the top, and inhaled that greasy, glorious meal as if we were two *Naked and Afraid* contestants who had just finished a forty-day challenge in the jungles of Ecuador, where all we'd ingested was a handful of barbecued termites and some boiled pond water. The salt and fat and who knows what other sacred, secret ingredients were in there woke us up, revived us. It tasted so damn good. It was a moment of pleasure after so many moments spent feeling like a hollowed-out husk, going through the motions, dreading, basically, everything. How did Meredith know? Had someone brought KFC to her door when she was feeling sad? Was it her go-to culinary pick-me-up? She was a genius, as far as I was—and am—concerned. Not just for the bucket of chicken, but for having the sense and the sensitivity to leave us in peace. The joy was temporary, our grief annihilated for a brief moment, but it is something I will never forget, that permission to forget, if only for the time it took to eat a few drumsticks.

Kayla Stewart, an award-winning food writer and coauthor of the cookbook *Gullah Geechee Home Cooking: Recipes from the Matriarch of Edisto Island*, says that in her travels, she's seen food left as offerings to the gods and left at the gravesites of lost loved ones.

"Food is the center of life, and death," says Stewart, who splits her time between Houston and Harlem when she's not on the road. "I've dealt with grief personally in my life, and I've observed others doing the same. In my culture, the repast is essential—a moment after the funeral to find fuel, restoration, and familial love and comfort in one room. If a neighbor or community member dies, you can expect stacks of casseroles to be delivered to the person's home—a kind Southern gesture that aims to soothe through taste. Food can be synonymous with culture, with pride, with safety, all emotions and themes that come up during loss."

We didn't have what you could call a feast after my mom's funeral, but we had a gathering at my cousin Jill's home. I don't have any recollection of the food that was there. I know we said some Hebrew prayers with the rabbi. I recall that we ate something, or at least I think we did. Jill would not have people over without putting out some sort of spread. What I remember the most is being surrounded by familiar faces—family, old friends, people we hadn't seen in years or even decades but who were so much a part of our childhood and our mom's life that it felt like no time had passed at all.

This was before Covid, so the memory and the experience of being surrounded by people who loved my mom was and is a positive, but, of course, bittersweet, one. There were no masks, no distance, no handshake anxiety. There were plenty of hugs, reassuring touches, and a physical closeness without fear of infection, which is a privilege that I hope I will never take for granted again. After weeks of isolating, voluntarily, in our pain, we finally wanted, and needed, other people. We needed their words and their warmth. We needed their stories and their food. We felt every ounce of love and compassion in that room, and it helped sustain us and push us forward on a day when we could have, would have, simply retreated. We welcomed every word, every gesture. We ate it up.

Chapter 4
Why Is This Geico Commercial Making Me Cry?

Seeing Reese Witherspoon glide down the Academy Awards red carpet in a Christian Dior halter-neck gown might not seem like a devastating experience worthy of a thousand salty tears. The "In Memoriam" segment at an awards show might be an obvious and appropriate time to weep, but what about that moment when Brad Pitt finally won a Best Supporting Actor award? Is it odd that I was crushed? I didn't need Joe Pesci to win, it's just that seeing Brad Pitt up there, with his movie star aura and his aw shucks hotness, made me miss my mom.

My mother adored Brad Pitt, from the moment she saw him in *Thelma and Louise*. How could she not? His gorgeousness in that movie is an objective fact at this point. I'm confident that his ripped torso is forever burned into the brains of millions of viewers. Beyond that, my mom never missed watching an awards show or a red carpet. After a few teenage years spent rebelling against her love of Hollywood glam, I accepted my fate and willingly inherited her obsession. Some people go to yearly Clippers games or spring training with their parents. They trade recipes or build things with power tools and bond over their ability to use a miter saw. As for me, I watched red carpets with my mom, every year, without fail, whether we were sitting side by side or texting from two thousand miles away.

> I need the TV from 1 p.m. until 11 p.m.
> It's the Oscars!

Jerett got used to receiving this exact text from me each year, warning him that our one television set was off-limits to him when an "important" awards show was on. He knew it was my time to watch celebrities twirl around for the slow-motion glam cam, but, more than that, it was my time with my mom. I loved texting back and forth with her, getting her hilarious and wry comments about the best and worst dressed. She died in November 2018, right before awards season kicked off. I spent much of December and January that first year worrying and wondering if I should watch the Golden Globes and Oscars and SAG and BAFTA and Independent Spirit Awards (we were not kidding around), or avoid them completely. I was afraid that the Dior gowns and acceptance speeches wouldn't dazzle me, but would gut me instead. It seems silly, but, in a way, obsessing over this seemingly meaningless decision helped me focus on something other than my actual pain. My heart was broken, but wait! The more pressing crisis was deciding whether or not

I should judge someone for wearing a pink tulle hoop skirt. In the end, that first year without my mom, I decided to watch. Jerett, who had avoided red carpets each year by using his own miter saw in the garage or by going to Home Depot for hours to buy teak oil and 200-grit sandpaper, actually sat with me and tried his best to fill the void by commenting on the outfits.

"That dress is . . . good? It's red."

"Why is there only one sleeve on that one? What's wrong with it?"

"Why is that diamond so big? I don't think that's even real."

He had nothing on my mother when it came to his commentary, and he didn't even know what a crinoline was, so I quickly put him out of his misery and told him I was fine and didn't he have something to hammer or sand in the garage anyway? He happily disappeared and I watched with my then–one-year-old son as my trusty companion. He, unlike Jerett, mercifully shared zero opinions about fashion.

The anticipation of watching the shows turned out to be much worse than the actual experience. I got through it and even had a little fun, but I was also sorrowful, of course. It was painful to look at my phone and sense the absence of my mom's texts. Unlike in years past, there was weight to this red carpet watching. It had a purpose beyond pure escape. It was the opposite of escape. This was diving headfirst, intentionally, into something that I knew would not just remind me of my mom's humor, but of her absence.

Some sweet friends texted me during the show, as they still do each year, telling me they were thinking of me and commenting on dresses, in an attempt to fill the silence. Those are the gestures, the seemingly small things that mean so much. No one needs to save you or make the pain go away or send you to Bali for three months; they just need to reach out and say, "Thinking of you. Did you see that neon-green *cape* he was wearing?"

Their comments would never rival my mom's, but they helped.

Watching the shows so soon after her death actually helped me feel close to my mom, as I imagined what she'd say about each sculptural stiletto or twinkling jewel. At least she, unlike my husband, would know that there is no way in hell Lady Gaga would be given a fake diamond to wear, whether she was going to the Oscars to accept an award or to Costco to buy a bag of potatoes. If you build something up to the point that you're prepared for the worst, it can sometimes end up feeling like nothing more than tiny daggers bouncing off a titanium shield. Often it's the unexpected moments, the ones that come out of nowhere when you're unarmed and unprepared, that hurt the most.

"Loss is so raw at the beginning," says Dr. Katherine Shear, head of Columbia University's Center for Prolonged Grief. "To adapt to a loss you have to accept the reality. It takes time to find a way for it to live in our house."

By watching those awards shows, I was trying to accept a new reality, one without my mom, the person who inspired me to care about them in the first place. I expected to break down, but I didn't. The real challenges became the surprise attacks. The moments when grief creeps up on you.

"It just hits when you least expect it" is a phrase that's become common between me and my dad each time we talk about the moments of randomly bursting into sobs or suddenly becoming mired in melancholy.

If a "news alert" with some juicy celebrity gossip like Bennifer's Second Act pops up on my phone, it's a reminder that I cannot text it to my mom to get her hot take. Every time I pass an antiques store, I release a painful sigh, because I'm reminded of the days she'd drag me to flea markets as a kid. What I would not give to be dragged, kicking and screaming, to flea markets with her now. At first, these triggers and buttons seem to be everywhere, whether they're obvious or completely unexplainable. I've cried during Geico commercials, not because my mom loved Geico, but because maybe it happened to be on TV at the exact moment that a suppressed burst of sorrow based on something that happened earlier that day needed to push forth and release itself. Or maybe she did love Geico and I just forgot. We carry around so many more emotions and hold so much more weight than we realize when we're newly grieving. The heaviness sneaks in without an invitation and stays a while, and it's easy to forget how much lighter you felt before this intruder appeared.

Maybe that's why we find ourselves weeping while watching an ad for auto insurance that somehow reminds us of our lost loved one, even though they never sold insurance and didn't even own a car.

If you do find yourself sobbing while watching an ad for dish soap, just remind yourself that grief, like life, doesn't always have to make sense. It's often unpredictable, intense when you expect a sniffle, and gentle when you're anticipating a body slam.

Marian Mankin from the bereavement center Bo's Place told me about one person in a grief group who told her that they unexpectedly burst into tears driving home one day, simply because of the way the light was hitting the trees.

"They had no idea why they were crying, and it can be very unsettling to have that feeling of, *What just happened?*" she says. "In the early days of grief, sometimes there is no emotional buffer between you and the world, and so commercials that might normally seem sappy suddenly make you have a full-out messy cry. Everything is so intense and raw. Your brain is processing so much in ways you don't even know."

Six months after my mom died, Jerett, Cole, and I left California and moved to my home state of Texas, a state I never thought I'd return to. As a teenager, you could have shot me out of Texas in a cannon and I would have been ecstatic. Grief has a way of bringing priorities into sharp focus, though, and

I felt a strong need to be near my dad and my sisters. I longed to return to my roots. It was a major life change, but, at that time, change was exactly what I needed.

One Saturday, two years after my mom died, my dad came to visit us in Hutto, where we were living, just north of Austin. Part of my new reality was spending much more time with my dad. We asked him to visit often, since we knew he was alone at home, surrounded by memories of my mom. I wanted to see him, too, more than ever. Losing one parent reminds you of how precious the time is, and being with my dad became a priority. Not a duty, but something vital to my happiness.

Enough time had passed that my dad and my sisters and I were functioning in the world, back to work, and settling into our new reality, instead of waking up each day confused and wondering how it was possible that my mom was not there. We were still rattled, and nothing was the same, but we were *functioning*. On this particular Saturday, I was sitting outside at a restaurant with my dad and Cole. A band was playing and we were having a good time, not talking about sad things, just listening to the music and drinking our beers. An upbeat country song came to an end, and the band launched into a cover of Stevie Nicks's "Landslide." Neither of us had any memories of that song linked to my mom, but as the band played on, my dad and I grew silent and our beers sat untouched. I felt heavy, on the verge of tears, destroyed. Do you know how beautifully, painfully sad the lyrics to

"Landslide" are? Can you listen to that song and not cry? And, if so, how? Elmo from *Sesame Street* could screech "Landslide" into a microphone and it would still be utterly heartbreaking. Bands should give some sort of trigger warning before they play it is all I'm saying.

Without uttering a word, my dad and I exchanged a look and we knew exactly, completely, how the other person felt. Any lightness we'd been feeling turned oppressive, without warning. My throat tightened, the way it gets when you're struggling to choke back rogue emotions. The laughter surrounding us sounded far off and strange. Was everyone else not hearing this? What would it be like to be one of those people unaffected by that song in that moment, not thinking of my mom, not struggling to breathe as if your chest had just been pummeled by a heavyweight? Not fighting the tears that were dangerously close to destroying every ounce of composure you'd worked so hard to maintain.

I looked at my dad and saw tears lurking around the edges of his eyes. One thing about losing a parent is having to see your other parent hold that sadness, too. I hated it, and still do. I can't stand seeing my dad cry, which he has often, thank goodness. As thankful as I am that he doesn't suppress how he's feeling, it's hard to watch. In some ways the roles change and you feel like a parent to *your* parent, worrying about their emotional well-being, wondering if they're eating enough or sleeping enough or being social enough. It can't be helped. It's just one of the many side effects of grief, worrying about the people you love, because you know their pain so well.

"Well, that was a lot," my dad said when the song ended, wiping away his tears.

"I know," I said. "Are you okay?" Of course he wasn't okay. Neither of us were.

They take a lot out of you, those unexpected moments. They don't care what time it is or what you're doing, whether you're about to lead a meeting or feed a child. They pay no attention to time zones or responsibilities. They're tactless and stealthy. They're also unavoidable. Not just because they strike without warning, but because, according to most experts, it's better to face them than push them away. As painful as they can be, it's better to let them in.

Grief therapist Ajita Robinson says that one negative that comes out of not facing the tough moments is that "You run the risk of being frozen in grief, and that becomes unhealthy. It doesn't give you a chance to metabolize grief and process a post-loss life." People sometimes overcompensate by trying to control things in their life, since grief and loss feel so out of their control. "It compromises the overall quality of life when we don't engage in the grief process," Robinson says. "When you're trying to heal, you may as well participate in that process."

Besides those moments when you're listening to "Landslide" and struggling not to slip into an emotional abyss, there's the numbness to contend with. In the months after my mom, and then, later, Jackie, died, I would catch myself feeling, basically, nothing. It worried me. How could nothingness feel so awful? What kind of a raw deal is that? In grief, you're either distraught or, if you're not distraught, you're feeling guilty that you're *not* feeling tormented.

Robinson calls the numbing aspect "a natural and normal part" of grief. It happens frequently in the immediate aftermath of loss. She says that it's "adaptive," in that it allows you to function and get through your daily routine, especially if you're a caregiver and you have to plan a funeral or take care of a child, or both. It's necessary, but it also shouldn't cause you to dissociate completely from experiencing grief because it just "kicks the can down the road." The emotions don't go away simply because you ignore them.

The numbness can make you feel like there is something deeply wrong with you because you are not doubled over sobbing every second of the day. My dad is no psychologist (he sells steel coils), but he is basically an expert on grief at this point. His theory is that we temporarily go numb to survive the pain. It helps us function for a while before the next wave slams us back. I also think that after experiencing such deeply felt, traumatic emotions, everyday existence tends to be mistaken for numbness. You're spent, cried out, wrung dry. A baseline, whatever your baseline is, can feel like you're flatlining, when really you're just at your baseline. I've learned that the experience of feeling guilty about feeling nothing doesn't seem to last long, so don't worry. Another session of gut-wrenching tears is probably right around the corner!

Numbness or detachment can also be a sign of prolonged grief, which is a state of heightened mourning that can actually be harmful. It can stop you from getting back into life, and doing things like going to work or seeing friends. Shear, head of Columbia's Center for Prolonged Grief, says, "Prolonged grief disorder means there is an initial, all-encompassing kind of grief. We like to say that grief emerges naturally and finds a place in your life; it doesn't disappear. Prolonged grief is when it just stays in a domineering role in your life and it interferes with your ability to move forward in a way that's meaningful." Periods of what might feel like emotional numbness, though, can be "a very natural coping mechanism." Shear says some troubling signs are when people feel disconnected from work, friends, or things that used to bring them joy. They don't feel okay moving forward or doing positive things for themselves, even after months or years. Prolonged Grief Disorder was added to the DSM-5 (Diagnostic and Statistical Manual of Mental Disorders, fifth edition) in 2022, and it caused some controversy, mainly because some people felt it was pathologizing grief. If it helps someone who is truly suffering, and they can get their insurance to cover treatment or medications, though, I'm all for it.

When Jackie died, I spent the first few weeks doing my share of weeping, gasping for breath, and painfully emoting everywhere I went. I tried to put on a smile for my son, but when I spoke to friends I could hear my voice shake. I felt weak, hollowed out. The barrier between me holding it together and me falling apart was about as precarious as a Victorian teacup with an anvil hanging overhead. But then, after a month or so, something strange happened. The breakdowns stopped and the anvil disappeared. I went on autopilot.

It's not as if I forgot. Jackie was on my mind every day. Her photos surrounded me. I conjured her voice in my mind at will, just because. Still, it all felt unreal, as it had that night on the plane when I found out she was gone. Amy's text saying I CAN'T BELIEVE THIS IS REAL came to define my everyday existence. I also started to worry about the numbness, or about the fact that I wasn't in turmoil every moment. I could go to restaurants or laugh at a movie. I could function, and this entry into "normal" life seemed to happen so much more quickly this time around, whereas with my mom it took about two years. Keep in mind, "normal" is all relative. Basically, I started to wonder why those early weeks of feeling distraught about my sister seemed to disappear so quickly. It didn't seem right. In other words, WHAT WAS WRONG WITH ME?

We found out that Jackie passed away on March 1. Her birthday was coming up on September 13, and, for months, from about April to September, I had been coasting. Sad, of course, but coasting. I had been through this before, though, so as her birthday approached, I braced for impact. I knew that Mother's Day and Thanksgiving and Halloween, which was my mom's birthday, had been tough, so I thought that September 13 might possibly obliterate the numbness and mercifully bring me back to the land of the disconsolate.

The morning of Jackie's birthday, I didn't wake up sobbing. I took Cole to school, and then drove to my appointment with an allergist. As a kid, I'd done the allergy testing where they prick your skin and drop different concoctions into the slit (probably not the correct medical explanation but bear with me), to see if you're allergic to ragweed or Pampas grass. Lucky me, I was allergic to pretty much anything that bloomed or grew in nature. Now here I was as an adult, back at the allergist to find out why I'd spent the summer sneezing and coughing and drowning my eyes in soothing drops. There is a thing in Texas called "cedar fever," and many of us live in fear of it, in case you're unfamiliar with how brutal allergies can be in this state. What I'm saying is, I itched.

It was a gray, cloudy morning. The kind of weather that would probably make me feel melancholy even if I'd just won a Super Lotto. I thought of Jackie more than usual. I thought of her intentionally, with purpose. This was the first birthday in forty years that I couldn't reach out to her. Even during the years when she was drinking and in horrible shape, years we weren't talking much because it's sometimes too painful to try to force closeness with an alcoholic when they're just not capable and it hurts too much, I would always at least send a text. Whether she texted back depended on her state at that moment. It didn't matter. I loved my sister, and no matter how enraged or frustrated I would become, I always wished her a happy birthday. And now I just couldn't, the same way I couldn't text my mom about the red carpet. As I drove to the allergist, that dawning reality that she was not there to reply or not reply to my text brought every emotion to the surface, every stored-up ounce of pain. The numbness was indeed obliterated, and the tears broke through. As soon as I pulled into a parking spot at the clinic, I called my dad.

"Dad, I'm sad about Jackie."

"I know. It just hits when you least expect it," he said, yet again.

This time, though, I did expect it. It was her birthday, after all. I guess that after so many months of coasting, I just didn't know it would hit this hard. How could I walk into a crowded waiting room and check in for my pinprick appointment when I could barely speak through my sobs? Even with a mask on, people would see that something was not right with me. As I sat in that car and stared at people coming and going through the double doors to the clinic, there was nothing unreal or surreal or hard to believe about Jackie's death. This was as real as you could get. This was hot tears, disgusting snot, red-blotches-on-your-face real. This was knowing someone is gone, feeling it to your core, understanding that there is nothing you can do to bring them back. This was the depths of grief. This was hell.

"It just hurts so much, Dad."

"I know honey. It happens to all of us."

In a way, I think I was almost relieved to have these feelings again, and to know that numbness was just me living in the world. It didn't mean I didn't love her, or miss her. It didn't mean there was something wrong with me, like my emotions had malfunctioned or that I was a coldhearted automaton. Despite the pain, or more likely because of it, I also felt how much I loved my sister in that moment. That feeling was just as real as the tears.

I told my dad I had to go, and apologized for making him sad, as if he weren't already sorrowful on his daughter's birthday, and every day. I got out of the car and didn't care if I looked like a troll who'd just wandered out of a dark cave where I'd been cursed to weep for an entire century. I figured that the doctor would just mistake my bloodshot eyes, splotchy skin, and hoarse voice for allergies. And if I did break down again while she was explaining cedar fever and pollen counts, I could just tell her the truth. I could tell her that my sister died on March 1, and today was her birthday. I could tell her that a day like this can be triggering, buttons can be pushed, but, despite all that, I'd live through it, and please keep talking about the pollen. I could just say I missed my sister, and that would be enough.

Chapter 5
It's a Sign

In the sixteenth century, Queen Elizabeth I had a court astrologer and scientific adviser named John Dee. Allegedly, in addition to gossiping with royalty about Mercury being in retrograde, Dee studied the occult. One day, maybe over a tipple of mead, he showed the queen an obsidian "spirit mirror" that he believed could help her see ghosts and apparitions reflected through the volcanic glass. The mirror now sits on display at the British Museum, and in an academic paper published in late 2021, researchers revealed that they were able to trace the mirror's origins to Aztec culture. How the British Dee got the mirror, which originated in Mexico, is a mystery. Maybe he obtained it via a clandestine black market deal on a trip to Bavaria, while wearing a cape. In any case, the Aztecs believed these mirrors were portals to the spirit world. Apparently, Queen Elizabeth I believed it, too.

My first encounter with someone who thought you could connect with spirits did not involve a centuries-old obsidian mirror or even a Ouija board. It involved butterfly hair clips worn by Ms. Boudreaux, my middle school art teacher.

There is always that one eccentric teacher whose offbeat habits cause a thousand ridiculous rumors to ricochet through the hallways of middle school. Mine was Ms. Boudreaux, devout wearer of butterfly hair clips, butterfly jewelry, and butterfly print clothing 365 days a year. Or at least she wore them nine months of the year. Maybe during the summer she ditched the jewelry and prints and switched to plain caftans. Based on her sartorial commitment throughout the school year, though, I highly doubt it.

The rumor was that Ms. Boudreaux's husband had passed away, and she believed that he was reincarnated as a butterfly. In addition to the butterflies, she also wore a stack of bracelets up each arm, and that fashion crime spawned a rumor that she believed that if she took off a single bracelet, someone else would die. There is a definite possibility that we had all watched too many scary movies, causing us to turn Ms. Boudreaux's clothing choices into a Hollywood horror plot. Or maybe these particular rumors were actually true. I searched for Ms. Boudreaux so I could ask her, but she's nowhere to be found.

Regardless of the rumors, I do remember Ms. Boudreaux sporting a questionable number of bracelets and butterflies. I also remember her throwing a ruler across the room in class one day. Having since experienced motherhood and the tyranny of incorrigible young kids, I completely understand her need to release a little stress by hurling a measuring stick through the air. Back then, we all thought Ms. Boudreaux was "crazy" and "weird." At that age, I couldn't empathize with her because my brain wasn't fully formed and the only grief I had experienced at that point was finding one of my Barbie dolls beheaded. Now, though, I understand Ms. Boudreaux, at least a little bit.

For millennia, humans have "seen" or communed with or sensed the dead. Whether you take this literally and visit a psychic medium, pull out your Ouija board so you can ask your grandmother for her secret lemon icebox pie recipe, or see someone in a dream, staying connected with those we've lost is one way to cope, and maybe even celebrate them. Look at Día de los Muertos in Mexico, or All Soul's Day in Italy, where the traditional cookie is called *ossa dei morti*, or bones of the dead. Today, most psychologists believe in "continuing bonds," and they promote a healthy attachment to the people we mourn. That could be talking to them at their gravesite, driving their old pickup truck, or, like my old art teacher, covering yourself in butterflies.

Columbia's Dr. Katherine Shear says you can stay connected to the person you've lost through those continuing bonds. "It's important to find a way to have that relationship in an ongoing way after someone has died," she says. "That's part of accepting grief into your life."

A 2013 study published in the *Journals of Gerontology* on the afterlife beliefs of widows and widowers found that some sort of spiritual continuing bond, whether it's a belief in reincarnation or some other sense of an afterlife or connection post-loss, can be "universally protective" for a bereaved person. Of the 319 participants who lost a spouse during the study period, 68 percent said they believed in an afterlife where loved ones are reunited. This kind of hope can sometimes help you feel like the person you're missing isn't gone forever, that your relationship with them is still part of your life. Having a spiritual belief system surrounding death isn't a prerequisite for learning to live with grief, but believing that a sudden rainstorm means your late husband is watching over you sounds pretty comforting, so why not look for signs and symbols, if that helps.

I wore my mom's cobalt-blue colon cancer awareness bracelet every single day for over two years after she died. It was a "linking object," something that belonged to her, that helped me feel connected. If it accidentally fell off, I would panic and frantically search until I found it again. I didn't think anything bad would happen, but *something* panicked me about losing it. It wasn't a superstition as much as a type of continuing bond. That piece of circular blue rubber that said NO ONE FIGHTS ALONE linked me to my mother, and reminded me of what she had endured. Eventually, after two and a half years of wearing it, I did lose that bracelet. One day I looked down and noticed that it was gone, but this time, my search wasn't frantic. I heard my mom's voice in my mind, saying, "Honey, stop wearing that ugly old bracelet and put on some pretty jewelry. It's time to move on." She (or I?) didn't mean move on *from her*, but from that bracelet. Letting go of that object felt right, at that time. It took a while to get there, but I was ready. Also, I just couldn't find it, which, looking back, may have been a sign in itself.

When my mom was sick, she would sometimes tease us by saying, "I'm going to come back and haunt you girls." Our response was always, "Please do." When she died, my sisters and I each waited for her to haunt us. We actually get a little jealous if one of us is "haunted" by our mom or Jackie in a dream. If she popped up now and then in an obsidian mirror to gossip or tell us to put on some lipstick, I would be thrilled, after the initial terror and shock wore off. That doesn't happen, obviously, as hard as I might wish for it. The night we found out Jackie died, my dad had a dream that he saw my mom standing in a white dress, looking sad and alone. It's the only visitation he's had from her, and it rattled him, seeing her so lonely. I told him I thought it was her telling him that she's there with him, mourning Jackie alongside him, and that *he* is not alone. I don't know if my interpretation is true, but it's more comforting than his take.

My friend Alisa Weinstein, whose father was kidnapped by al-Qaeda in 2011 and killed in 2015, told me that several months after her father died, she went to a medium to try to connect with him. It's something I've thought about doing, but I haven't mustered the courage to try just yet. This could be because at a party during my junior year of college, a guy named

Gabriel told me he was psychic, so I let him read my palm in an apartment stairwell. Instead of telling me I would make millions and meet the love of my life in the south of France, he told me that I was going to die by the age of thirty. Thankfully, Gabriel did not have the "gift." That stairwell encounter disturbed me so much, though, that a few years later, when I went into the home of a psychic in San Francisco for a reading, I actually ended up fleeing before the woman could even begin. I had not turned thirty yet, so Gabriel's words echoed in my ears, driving me away from the crystal ball and out into the street. I guess that's all to say I'm still scared to visit a psychic medium. Alisa told me that readings and mediums were not something she previously believed in, but she missed her dad and desperately wanted to "see" him in some way. Lucky for Alisa, her experience wasn't as upsetting as mine was. Her biggest takeaway was that the medium told her that when she or her mom saw a gathering of birds, that would be her dad.

"I was skeptical at first," Alisa says. "But a few months later I went to visit my mom and we noticed all of these birds gathered in an azalea bush outside her house, so we were like . . . maybe it's Dad." She says birds are now a way for her to feel her dad close to her. "I'll be walking in downtown San Francisco and a hummingbird will dart in front of me and I'm like, 'Hi Dad,'" she says. "I know it's ridiculous, but it just gives you a moment to think of them, for whatever that might be worth."

I swear I saw my paternal grandmother Nana sitting in a chair in the corner of my college bedroom once. I woke up in the middle of the night, and there she was, calmly watching me. There was no fear or shock. I didn't call a paranormal inspector. Instead, I felt at peace, as if she were there to protect me. I cherish that memory. Did I hallucinate her, because I missed her at that moment? Was I just seeing things during a late-night college haze? To me, she was there, and that's all that matters.

Joyal Mulheron from the bereavement nonprofit Evermore says that snowfall is the sign that helps her feel her daughter Eleanora's presence. On the one-year anniversary of Eleanora's death, it snowed, which Mulheron says is uncommon for Washington, DC in October. When she later delivered her son, it snowed for the twenty minutes he was being born. Now, snowfall always connects her to the daughter she lost, and brings her comfort, even in her sorrow. She also has an urn holding Eleanora's ashes in the house, which her son has covered in Spider-Man stickers.

"He has become quite connected to her," she says of her son and daughter. "It's a way of integrating her into our lives. It's those little things you have that you try to hold onto that help you make it to the next day."

My mom might not literally haunt us, but she has visited my youngest sister Kathryn, apparently many times. After the funeral, Kathryn started sending photos of butterflies to the family text chain, which consists of my dad, my sisters, and myself. She would follow the photos with texts like:

It's Mom!

I was not aware of how many different butterflies there are in Texas until I started getting these near daily texts from Kathryn. Photos of Monarchs that read LOOK, IT'S MOM! Or maybe an image of a Painted Lady butterfly, simply accompanied by: MOM! My dad, Amy, and I wouldn't discourage Kathryn's texts, because we knew it brought her comfort, and it helped us, too. She did stretch our beliefs one day when the butterflies turned into something less ethereal.

IT'S MOM I SWEAR!

And then, I guess to explain why she was texting us a blurry photo of a rooster:

SHE ALWAYS LOVED ROOSTERS

This random rooster ran across Kathryn's path when she was jogging one day in Houston, and she was convinced that a rogue male chicken had something to do with our mom. Or that it was our mom. At that point, the butterfly and rooster texts became a running joke, but one we still treated with respect. We were laughing *with* her, cheering her on. We longed to be in the presence of our mom, too, so we understood the need to seek her out anywhere you could. I don't know if that rooster was my mom reincarnated, but if my sister wanted to believe it was, then who was I to tell her it wasn't? We did have a lot of rooster figurines in the kitchen growing up, so who knows.

"It's important to honor each individual journey," says Tony Pham, the meditation teacher and death doula. "Just like in *The Matrix*, if your mind thinks it's real, then it's real."

We see our loved ones in double rainbows and cardinals and sudden thunderstorms, and in moments when sunlight breaks through the clouds. They appear in dreams and lamp-light flickers and an unexpected cool breeze. Maybe the visitations and bracelets and rituals are our way of keeping the love we felt and feel for the person we lost burning. It's also a way of convincing ourselves that they're okay. And when we decide to let things go, like a blue bracelet or a butterfly hairpin, *if* we decide to let them go, it doesn't mean we're grieving less, but that we've learned to coexist with grief in a new way.

A study of Japanese widows showed that their continuing bonds, in the form of lighting candles or leaving out food for the dead, actually help them find strength in the face of grief. I don't leave cheese plates or chocolate out for my mom and sister, but I do toast them sometimes. On my desk, I have a photo of my sister Jackie, next to a small stained-glass lamp that my mom gave me, so in a way that's like a little shrine, and a way to keep them close. When I tuck my son in each night before bed, I list off the people who love him, and I always include "Cici and Aunt Jackie." Some nights, saying their names causes me to stop breathing for a moment, and I have to force myself to inhale and continue saying the words. My son will never know his maternal grandmother or my sister, so this ritual is my way of making them present for him, even if I'm simply saying their names. Hopefully, he'll know them through the stories I tell and the photos I show him, and he'll form his own bonds with them. They might even visit him in a dream. Maybe they already have.

Our connections to the dead are extremely personal, and they can help us make sense of life after loss. Not in a scientific way, since I don't think any of these practices can be quantified or examined in a petri dish, but, emotionally, they can bring some solace. If you're a nihilist, and if that life philosophy helps you process your pain, then you don't have to force yourself to imagine your loved one sitting on a puffy white cloud with a ukulele. Just tell yourself that nothing matters and life is a meaningless series of actions and events, and enjoy whatever it is that nihilists enjoy: Blank stares? A satisfying shrug? Pointlessly hurtling through space? When I think about the torrent of emotions that grief can bring, nihilism actually sounds pretty relaxing, but you can't force a life philosophy. I like believing that life does have meaning, and things do matter, even if that brings more uncertainty and pain.

There's an old European custom that's been traced back to Celtic mythology called "telling the bees," which I love. Bees have long symbolized the link between our world and the spirit world, and this tradition of "telling the bees" has been documented throughout Western Europe, and in parts of rural New England and Appalachia during the nineteenth century. If a death occurred, a family member would have to notify the beehive of the death. I guess back then everyone had a beehive at home, like we have Alexas. They would often drape the hives in a black cloth, or place a black cloth on a stick next to the hives. Failure to "put the bees into mourning" meant that more loss and death would occur. Over the years, painters captured this custom on canvas. John Greenleaf Whittier wrote an entire poem about the tradition, called, for good reason, "Telling the Bees." A Victorian biologist and author named Margaret Warner Morley writes about it in her book *The Honey-Makers*, in a chapter called "Curious Customs and Beliefs." It might not be widely practiced anymore, but it's not such a bad idea, if you have a beehive. When Queen Elizabeth II died in September 2022, the Royal Beekeeper went and told the palace bees, so in some circles, the tradition lives on. If whispering to the bees isn't your thing, you can choose to believe in signs like hummingbirds gathered over an azalea bush or roosters crossing your path. When you lose someone you love and yearn for their presence, it may be comforting to look to signs or symbols you once laughed off. As silly as my sister's moment with that renegade rooster might seem, I believe that if she *felt* that my mom was there in that moment, she was there. Sometimes, in grief, that's all the proof we need.

Chapter 6
Telling My "Safe Place" to Go to Hell

When tough things happen in life, we're often rewarded for showing Grit, with a capital "G." Also known as Resilience, Fortitude, Strength, and Perseverance. There are TED Talks about Grit, and books entirely devoted to the topic. Articles claim that children who exhibit Grit go on to rule the world, or at least become CEOs of start-ups, two occupations that some people tend to mix up. The hero of every great story exhibits Grit in some form, and their Resilience is what helps them overcome obstacles and make it to the denouement. In keeping with this widely held but deeply flawed belief system, I've always tried to tough things out, and handle whatever comes my way. I tried this with grief, too, but it didn't work out as planned.

My mom didn't use the word *grit* when I was a kid, since it wasn't yet a trendy catchword. It was more of a John Wayne silent cowboy on the range–type word back then. Instead, my mom would say, "Honey, there will always be someone taller, prettier, wealthier, and more successful than you. Now go get dressed." This tough love mantra drove me crazy as a teenager, but as I got older, I found myself continually reciting it in my mind whenever something upset me—a job I didn't land, a breakup, a layoff. It buoyed me when life or circumstances threatened to drag me down. It gave me strength, and I came to pride myself on that strength. Maybe a little too much.

The problem with pride is that it gets in the way, as they say. It can mask what's truly going on, and give you a false sense of feeling that you have everything under control. People praise you for handling it, so you assume you're handling it. It's not that I was a stoic lone wolf who didn't believe in or seek out therapy over the years. I went to a therapist in middle school, probably because the dark, maudlin poetry I was writing on my closet walls with a black Sharpie made my parents think I needed some help, when really I just loved poetry, and writing on walls was an early, pre-tattoo attempt at rebellion. I went to therapy again, on my own, right after college. This was to help with an existential crisis in my early twenties, which sent me reeling due to privileged thoughts like these: Who Am I? What Is the Meaning of Life? And How the Hell Do I Get Paid to Write in Paris Cafes All Day? I returned to therapy several years later after a rough breakup, and it helped tremendously. I understand that I cannot possibly handle everything on my own, but that doesn't mean I don't like to try. Dealing with loss, though, makes a mid-twenties meltdown or an ill-fated romance—painful as they may be in the moment—seem almost quaint. The aftereffects of deep grief can topple even the steadiest of stoics. Rogue emotions creep up on you, and attack at will. Pride doesn't stand a chance in that fight.

"People in general struggle with asking for help," says Marian Mankin of the Houston bereavement center Bo's Place. "They want to be strong for others or they don't want to burden others, and it might feel like the world is moving on without them. Someone might tell you you're strong, but you might feel like you're under duress, or feel like, 'What choice do I have? This is the reality of my life.'"

When I returned to Los Angeles after my mom's funeral, I went straight back to work. As Mankin says, what choice did I have? I unpacked my bags, cleaned the house, took Cole to day care, and drove the sixteen-mile, ninety-minute commute to my job. If that sounds like a miscalculation, you have probably never experienced LA traffic, where it can take half an hour to move one city block. Again, not a miscalculation. After my breakdown on day one of work, I went back and made it through each hour, sometimes with the help of a soul-crushing cry, but I always dried my tears and forged ahead. Los Angeles felt different to me, though. The sweet-scented paradise of my twenties had morphed into a city where the springtime jasmine and the random celebrity sightings could no longer distract me from the tragic flaws that were becoming more apparent now that I had a mortgage and a kid. It became a city where gas, home, and childcare prices were criminal. And so, two months after my mom died, my husband took a job in Texas, a state I had once fled.

California wasn't the shimmering oasis it once appeared to be, but completely uprooting my life so soon came as a shock. Where would we live? Was I quitting my job and updating my resume? Finding an affordable, non-terrifying day care in LA without a three-year waiting list had been a nightmare, and I wasn't sure I had the stamina to endure that *Hunger Games*-esque parenting challenge all over again. To give you a sense of how stressful it was, one Los Angeles day care I visited while pregnant told me that their records were "in the vault" when I asked them for a few references. This was an in-home day care with three rooms, broken toys, and sleeping bags on the floor, so I seriously doubt they had a secret, state-of-the-art vault where they kept Aiden's and Olivia's mommy's phone numbers. The thought of navigating America's childcare hellscape all over again depressed me. In many ways, my mind and body were still back in that hospice week, and still processing my mom's funeral, but the present and future kept tugging me along. So I created a barely legible spreadsheet and started googling day cares north of Austin.

It was fine, though. I would persevere. Look at me, handling it all! "I am woman, hear me not lose my shit," as Helen Reddy sort of sang. We had a one-year-old son and fifty-one steps to climb to the front door of the house. My mom was gone forever, my sister Jackie was back in detox, I had a boss who pretty clearly wanted me gone to make way for a twenty-two-year-old in designer mom jeans, and, oh yes, my family's future was thrown into chaos. But it would all work out, if I just showed some good old-fashioned grit, like trudging up those fifty-one steep steps while holding a child in one arm and groceries in the other, multiple times a day.

I tried, as hard as I could. In addition to day cares, I started researching jobs and rental homes. It made me feel good when people said, "I don't know how you're functioning!" Or "You're amazing, the way you're handling all of this. And those steps!" I would humbly say, "Well, life can be tough, but you just have to keep going," or some other bullshit line that, at the time, I thought I believed. Little did I realize, I was slowly, quietly, starting to fall apart. You can scream all you want about gender stereotypes, but the truth is that women shoulder everything, all the time. Do you know how hard it is some days to make dinner and fold laundry and feed children and go to work and grieve and wash the dishes and cry without completely unraveling? Women have been quietly exhibiting grit for centuries, which makes it even more of a head-scratcher that we don't run all the companies or have higher positions of power in general around the world in every industry known to humankind.

Anyway.

I thought the early days of losing my mother were hard, but the months that followed were difficult in ways I had not anticipated. I didn't understand what it meant to live with loss. I wondered, as so many do, when the crying and sadness and the urge to text or call her would end. I wanted to know when things might go back to "normal." When would I be able to listen to her voicemails that I saved and feel wistful, instead of utterly destroyed, to the point where I had to crawl into bed for a few hours to cope? How long would it take until it didn't seem "surreal" that my mom was not here? These questions have no answers, or at least the answers vary for everyone, on any given day. And so, for months, I pretended to have it all under control. I soldiered on, taking care of everything but myself.

I was scared to leave California and the semi-security of my job, but I was also excited to be a few hours' drive from my dad and sisters after so many years away. In Texas, we rented a single-story home that was three times the size of our Los Angeles "bungalow," and it had *one step* into the house from the attached garage. Cole's preschool was an actual, adorable school, and it was half the price we had been paying. They had splash-pad days in the summer, a farmer brought cows for them to milk, and no one mentioned a vault. In a major lifestyle upgrade, I was not commuting sixteen miles in ninety minutes. I was working from home, and not because of a pandemic, which was yet to upend the planet. These massive changes, plus the mundane duties that went along with them, like wrapping dishes in newspaper and packing up a home to move halfway across the country, provided temporary distractions. A few months after our move, though, about eight months after losing my mom, I started noticing that things were not right. I was not right.

Jerett and I were fighting, and the smallest things gave me anxiety or frustrated me, or both. Daily responsibilities helped mask the fact that I was, on some level, deeply pained. When I was alone, I talked to myself constantly. I think this started as a way for me to process even small daily disruptions, but it became a habit I could barely control. I talked to myself at home, in the car, at the grocery store, walking to the mailbox for all the neighbors to see. Talking to yourself can be a healthy way to process things, but this was compulsive. Plus these talks were often more like rants, about anything and everything that went something like this:

Can Jerett close a single cabinet or drawer in his entire life, just one time . . . Why is this truck driving twenty miles per hour the speed limit is seventy-five . . . No one else in this house cleans and I'm over it . . . Why are houses so expensive . . . I'm done with the news it's so depressing . . . This woman is in the Fifteen Items or Less lane and she has about forty things . . . I am not letting this truck over . . . This heat is horrible . . . Why is it so cold in this store . . . Why are the neighbors blaring Metallica at three in the morning . . . That asshole just threw a McDonald's bag out the window what is wrong with people . . . I am over this . . . I need to get away . . . I should start a gratitude journal . . . this gratitude journal is so dumb, all I write is that I'm thankful for coffee . . . I'm going to bed at eight o'clock tonight, I don't care what anyone says . . . I can't sleep . . . I'm exhausted . . . I'm done with this day.

That's just a small snippet of the gripes I would give voice to throughout the day. Even my sleep was stressful. I hadn't worked in restaurants in years, but I had repeated dreams about waiting tables and forgetting the orders. If that doesn't sound extremely upsetting, you have likely never waited tables. Getting yelled at because you forgot to bring the chive butter or the steak knife is not fun whether it's happening in real life, or in a dream.

When I wasn't ranting to myself, or having stress dreams, I caught myself snapping at Jerett, and then snapping at Cole, who wasn't even two years old. I was trying to handle it all, not even noticing that things were falling down around me, like too many piled-up boxes tumbling out of my arms.

In a 2011 study, conducted by researchers at the University of Texas at Austin and the University of Minnesota and published in the journal *Social Psychological and Personality Science*, the researchers found that bottling up your emotions in the moment led to more aggressive behavior. They had participants watch disturbing scenes from the Monty Python movie *The Meaning of Life* and from the film *Trainspotting*, and half were allowed to show their emotions and the other half had to repress them. The ones who weren't allowed to express their feelings later showed signs of stress and acting out, "by yelling at their children, perhaps." In an attempt to "handle it," I wasn't allowing myself to truly go there, emotionally, and let out all the anger, fear, sadness, and ten thousand other emotions swirling around inside of me. The last thing I wanted to be was a mom who yelled at her son every time he put his iPad volume too high or got pink slime stuck in his hair. I needed to unleash the pent-up jumble of rage inside me safely, away from my family. I needed professional help.

"I think I need to see someone," I finally told Jerett.

Another clue that I needed help was that I felt constantly on the verge of tears. I had become accustomed to a certain level of stress, so I was moving through the world in a heightened state of anxiety that I didn't even realize was anxiety. I came to believe that it was just how I was, how I'd always been. I had forgotten what "healthy" even felt like. I missed my mom, and I barely had time to mourn her since we were thrust into selling a house and moving and uprooting our life in a short period of time. Hard as I tried, I could not cope. I set out to find a therapist. After days of calls and emails, I found someone in Austin who took our insurance and who sounded kind and did not seem like they were going to hand me crystals and tell me to chant. I wasn't sure if this person would help, but I was willing to try. If it was the right decision, I'd know soon enough.

At the first appointment, I sat in the windowless waiting room, staring at the therapist's closed door. At first, I felt pretty calm. Maybe I had things at least a little bit under control after all. But then, out of nowhere, a stream of tears quietly unleashed themselves. Who knows what set me off. Maybe the thought that my mom worked as a receptionist in her twenties, just like the receptionist in this waiting room. Maybe the sweet painting of three kids riding bikes triggered something in me. As I struggled to contain the emotions kicking at the door of my false calm, the receptionist kept typing away. Between the clicks of her nails on the keyboard and the low hum of the little white sound machines strategically positioned at each office door, the room should have felt like a relaxing ASMR cocoon instead of an emotional torture chamber. I didn't want to cause a scene, so I tried some textbook deep breathing and got myself halfway settled. As soon as the therapist opened the door and asked me to come in, I bolted into the room and broke down. Therapy is probably the right decision if you find yourself sprinting into the office to unload a torrent of emotions onto a complete stranger, before you even say hello.

Carla, the therapist, handed me some tissues. She had a short blond pixie cut, and kept a navy blue cardigan draped

over her chair. The office was vibrant, with colorful draw-
ings that looked like they were made by young children
posted on the walls. She had thick plastic binders full of lit-
erature about anxiety and grief. I told Carla about my mom's
death and my sister's alcoholism. I told her I was snapping
at my husband and son, that I was angry at Jackie for not
pulling herself together enough to be with us that horrible
hospice week, and that I thought I could handle it all but
obviously I can't and grief is a beast and I don't know how to
fix that, and by the way I'm compulsively talking to myself
out loud in public so something is clearly wrong because I
cannot seem to stop.

"Do you have a safe place?" Carla asked. "Somewhere
you can picture in your mind that might be calming, when
you're feeling stress or anxiety?"

"Not right now," I said.

I knew about the concept, and I'd tried envisioning a
safe place over the years to ease my mind. I usually closed
my eyes and teleported to a field of tall moonlit grass, or to
waves gently crashing on a beach at night. Not utterly original safe places on my part, but I had never been to a Buddhist
monastery on the side of a remote mountain in Tibet, so I
used what I had. I told Carla that I'd been to various safe
places in my time, but it had been a while.

"Would you like to try finding one?"

"Sure."

I wasn't thrilled about the idea, but I was ready to try anything. It's also not in my nature to be blunt and direct, so, like many well-mannered Southerners, I tend to act agreeable rather than hurting someone's feelings, even if it means I have to do something I *really* would rather not do. It's a curse, one that's drilled into you from birth. My grandmother once gave me a leopard-print denim jacket with fringe as a birthday gift, and as soon as I opened it up and my mom saw the horrified expression on my preteen face, she shot me a look that very clearly said: *You put that jacket on right now and tell Mamaw you adore it and have never seen anything cuter in your life, or else.* So I did.

It wasn't Carla's fault. I'm sure if I would have told her I despised safe places, she would have been professional about it, instead of experiencing crippling self-doubt about her skills as a therapist. But, just as my sisters and I nodded and listened to Glyn's murder tale that first night of hospice and just as I put on that fringed leopard-print denim jacket, I nodded, closed my eyes, and traveled to a grassy field at night.

After a few seconds I realized that maybe a grassy field wasn't the right place. Maybe the ocean was the key this time. So I headed to the ocean, but it wasn't as relaxing as I'd hoped. My mom loved the sound of the waves, so now I was thinking about her, again. Where else could I go? Napa? A Tuscan villa? That seemed like a bit much. After a few seconds of frantic imaginary travel, I somehow ended up in the backyard of a pretty white clapboard house next to a creek. There was a grill outside and Jerett and Cole were playing in the dappled sunlight. It was idyllic, straight out of Zillow heaven. I had no idea where this home was, but I definitely wanted to live there. This safe place was alright.

"Tell me what you see and hear. What are the smells?" Carla asked.

I told her I was lounging alone on the grass, watching Cole and Jerett play. The sun was warm, the grass was soft, and the air smelled like . . . honeysuckle? Steaks on the grill? I tried as hard as I could to really go there, to be there, to transport myself to this rural paradise and let all my worries dissolve into dust and get carried away on a warm breeze, until I felt weightless, free, enveloped in warmth and love. It was wonderful, a great escape. There was just one problem.

I missed my mom.

The safe place faded in and out as I struggled to stay put, but it didn't stick around long enough for me to truly let go. That clapboard house by the creek *was* soothing. I did want to be there, very much. But as lovely as a place may be, there is no escape from grief. And even if there were, I didn't want it. I wanted to feel angry and I wanted to ask questions. I wanted to be able to say, *This isn't fair*, and have someone else say, *No, it's not*. I understand that safe places can be a crucial tool for coping with anxiety and trauma and even grief, but going to a pretty, calm place, be it an ocean or a field or a country cottage, was not bringing my mom back, or even giving me a mini break from stress. That realization actually upped my anxiety, instead of quelling it. I didn't tell this to Carla for several sessions, though. I just kept trying.

I was willing to do this because therapy takes time and commitment, so I committed to that damn clapboard house as if I were in escrow. I also knew that therapy "breakthroughs" don't happen overnight. Just think about any movie or show you've ever seen where the plot revolves around someone going to therapy. It takes them forever to have their moment. *Ordinary People*, *Good Will Hunting*, Nicole Kidman in *Big Little Lies*, Bill Murray in *What About Bob?* All these characters work like hell to reach some sort of realization or epiphany. I wasn't even sure what a breakthrough meant for me, though. Maybe it would be feeling less anxious and tense on a day-to-day basis. No matter how skilled and compassionate your therapist or grief counselor is, there's no formula for getting to the end, because there really is no end. There is just, maybe, less struggle, and a way forward. Maybe "the end" is the beginning of living side by side with grief, and allowing it to exist right there with you, not as something that keeps you in the past or drags you down, but as something that is integral to who you are now, because you are not the same. You can't be.

You're someone who understands, possibly for the first time, that love is not an emotion reserved for the heart. It's in your bones, your blood, your cells. It pierces every part of you. It's barbed wire, and a running stream. It will not save you, or make you appreciate every moment as if it were your last. But it might, at times, allow you to exist in your moment of pain, and remember where that pain is coming from. This might not happen in a dramatic breakthrough moment, and that realization—that it's coming from love—might not always make you feel warm and fuzzy. Sometimes it will piss you off, even make you hate love. But what is the point of all this living if we don't somehow hold and keep the people we've loved in our bones, in our blood, even, especially, when it hurts.

"We say as a society that you need to be resilient, but my thing is—let's cancel resilience," says Evermore's Joyal Mulheron. "Most of us experience hardships and the last thing we should be expected to hear is something like, 'Oh, your kid died? You should experience meditation.' I'm sorry, but it's not about resilience. It's about weathering."

After several sessions spent in Carla's office, closing my eyes and fading in and out of my safe place, I finally broke with Southern etiquette and told her it wasn't working for me. By "working" I meant my mind did not want to lounge on that grassy lawn, it wanted to drift to the grocery store aisles so I could make a mental shopping list for later. It wanted to park itself in this room with the little sound machine outside, and just talk about what was right in front of me, what was wrong, what ached. Carla was understanding, and said we didn't have to do the "safe place" again. We could just talk. I was relieved, until she pulled out a contraption that looked like it was straight out of a 1950s horror movie about psycho-analysis and asked me if I wanted to try EMDR (eye movement desensitization and reprocessing) therapy. EMDR was developed to treat PTSD (post-traumatic stress disorder), and it involves reliving past traumas and hearing clicking and tapping sounds as you do this. It's now used to treat all sorts of traumas, as well as things like anxiety and grief. EMDR may work for some, and in fact I know people who find that it helps them tremendously, including my father, but Carla was clearly not listening to my "I just want to talk about real shit" needs. And so, as gently as I could, I told her this, too, wasn't working out. She understood.

I searched and found a new therapist, and before our first session I made sure he understood that I did not want any safe places, taps, or clicks. I wanted to talk. And so, every Tuesday at noon for two years, we did just that. We talked—about grief, about parenting, about everything. One of the best things he said to me, when I told him how little patience I had for other people's daily complaints, was "This is common in grief. You often have zero tolerance for petty bullshit."

That was exactly right. This therapist was the one for me.

As Marian Mankin says of finding a therapist or grief group that feels right for your specific needs and experience, "You wouldn't take a Honda to a Ford dealership." Therapy is not one size fits all. It's also not a sure thing. It can help, though. My dad's grief group and his therapist have given him a place to go, real or virtual, where he can express himself and meet other people who understand. He says that sometimes, if he can maybe help someone else by just listening to them or sharing his own story, that in turn helps him. He wants to speak at meetings about my sister, and about what it's like losing a child to alcoholism. On some days he needs to cry, and not just to us. When my sister died, so soon after my mom, I did not think my dad would ever recover. He even told us, "I don't think I'll make it through this one." He's not the same, but he's here. Not just existing, but living, and full of love. I think that's largely because he reached out, instead of disappearing inward. With the 450 texts my sisters and I send him each day, it's pretty much impossible for him to retreat.

When I asked Mankin what she tells people who come to Bo's Place, but who might still be skeptical about getting help, she said, "If people are reluctant, I tell them that therapy isn't only about what's wrong. It's also about what can be better."

For me, better was not a moonlit field or the backyard of my imaginary dream home by a creek. It wasn't about feeling safe, or even content. Better was facing what was painful or infuriating. It was accepting that, even on a good day, a wonderful day, grief might knock me down, and that's how this would go. I should also add that I went on an SSRI (Selective

Serotonin Reuptake Inhibitor), because as my mom once said, "If I thought it would make me feel better, I would eat dirt if a doctor told me to." I stopped snapping at Jerett and Cole (well, most of the time). I kept up with therapy until I felt like I had said everything I needed to say in that room. I also still talk to myself, but I try to counter any negative rants with something positive, to even out the scales. Maybe one day I'll go back to therapy, but, for now, I'm trying to use what I learned on my own. Going back is a door I will never close.

I can't say whether or not I'll try out a "safe place" if I'm asked to again, or even EMDR, because you never know. The other day I actually eyeballed some healing crystals at a shop in Austin, but I refrained from buying one. By some strange coincidence, or maybe just by chance, we did end up leaving our rental and moving into a rural house by a creek. It's not white clapboard, but the grass is green, for a few months of the year at least. I can smell honeysuckle, sometimes. And, in this home that they'll never see, I think about my mom and my sister, always. There is not one major therapy break-through along the way that I can point to, but maybe there are small ones, each day, or once in a great while. Maybe the breakthrough is walking out onto the grassy lawn, not to escape or seek safety, but to ache for the people I've lost, and not be destroyed by the fact that they're gone. The break-through is being able to hold tighter to the love in that ache than to the pain.

Chapter 7
Mourning Them When They're Here, But Not

It was midmorning in Manhattan. I was walking up Fif-teenth Street, toward Fifth Avenue, heading to the upscale sushi restaurant where I worked. I was scheduled for a double that day, which meant that, for at least eight hours, I would be serving ebi, hamachi, and a slow-poached octopus that one critic called "outrageously good." There was a bodega on Fifth that I sometimes ran into before work to stock up on important contraband like gum, also known as a little piece of heaven that I was only allowed to chew between shifts. Just as I was getting close enough to turn the corner, there she was. Instead of calling out to her, I froze.

She crossed the intersection alone, wearing what seemed like clothes from the night before. Then again, she did always dress like a movie star, even if she was just heading to Wal-greens for some Chapstick. Her shock of bright burgundy hair made her impossible to miss. That hair had become her signature look. The wild color never ceased to frustrate our mom, whose philosophy was "The blonder, the better, espe-cially if you're brunette." Jackie wasn't trying to blend in, though. She loved glamour and drama, so maybe it was her way of making a statement or standing out.

On the day I saw her crossing Fifth Avenue, Jackie lived in Queens and I lived in Brooklyn, so the chances of us running into each other in Manhattan, at 11 a.m. in a city of over eight million people, seemed slim. I'd only been there for a few months, and it was the first time my sister and I had lived in the same city since I was in high school. I had decided to leave California for New York right after graduate school, not for fortune or fame, but for love. My stay only lasted one year, and during that time, the severity of my sister's alcoholism was something I could no longer ignore. If our relationship were "normal," if I knew then what I know now, I would have called her name that day in the street, run to her, hugged her. If things were different, we would have laughed about how random and strange and lucky this was. Instead of yelling her name, though, I prayed she wouldn't see me. As quickly as she appeared, Jackie disappeared into the mass of people coming and going, never knowing that her eldest sister was standing ten feet away, looking right at her. Instead of going to the bodega, I turned back and headed into work.

That encounter haunts me. Years went by, and I never told Jackie that I saw her that day. I didn't tell most people, since explaining the complexities of loving an alcoholic to anyone who hasn't lived it can be challenging. How could I not say hello to my own flesh and blood? The baby sister who slept in my bed when she was little, because she was scared to sleep alone. Was I cruel, intolerant, devoid of sympathy? It wasn't my sister crossing the intersection that day, though. It was the person she became when her addiction took over, and that person had flaked on lunches and dinners for months, without texting or calling, making up excuses that didn't add up, and sending me into an anxiety spiral as I constantly worried about whether she was okay, or even alive. That person disappeared, and reemerged when she needed something. I didn't know how to talk to that person without my heart breaking, and without becoming filled with rage that this was where we had ended up, and that she couldn't do the simplest things, like show up.

When we did manage to meet up, it was often at the Whole Foods in Union Square, a few blocks from my job. It was an easy commute for me and I figured that if Jackie did flake, I would at least be close to the restaurant where I worked. We'd meet out front, pick our food, and then take the escalator to the second floor to eat. I remember riding behind her one day, looking out the tall glass windows to the crowded streets outside, and then up at Jackie, inches in front of me, yet feeling so far away. We didn't talk on the ride up. My stomach was in knots, which I now recognize as anxiety. Back then, my nerves just confused me, and the confusion, in turn, made me angry. Why did it have to be so hard, just to come face-to-face with my own sister? When we did sit down to eat, the conversation centered on her complaints, her job as an aesthetician, her status as the forever victim.

"My boss hates me."

"Why do you think she hates you? Didn't you just get a raise?"

"She's a bitch. She's always accusing me of being late, and I'm not."

"Why is she accusing you? Can't you talk to her?"

"No. She hates me. She's crazy."

When Jackie was not sober, she never asked about my job or my relationship. If I brought anything up about my life, she'd switch right back to talking about herself. By the end of these conversations, I would almost wish she would have flaked. I'd leave rattled, a jumble of nerves, wondering where my sister had gone, and why it was so hard to relate to the person right in front of me.

I was not the victim here. I don't want it to seem that way at all. In this type of relationship, we are all victims, in a sense—the addicts and the ones who love them. We are all in pain, and it can take years, or a lifetime, to get a handle on our experiences, and the anguish we've each felt. The hurt runs deep on both sides, but it might take time to fully real–ize that, and to give the other person grace. It took me years.

In this type of relationship, we grieve for the person when they're gone, but also when they're here. I never knew to call it grief when my sister was alive, though.

In the 1970s, psychologist and author Dr. Pauline Boss coined the term "ambiguous loss" when she was interviewing the wives of pilots who were missing in action during the Vietnam War. She's written several groundbreaking books and hundreds of papers about the topic, and her research has helped people who have struggled to understand why they experience feelings of grief when death is not the catalyst. Ambiguous loss is the pain experienced by the loss of a loved one who is still alive, accompanied by the death or a change in the relationship. When my sister was alive, her alcoholism fundamentally changed our relationship, but it took me years to realize that I was grieving the relationship we had before. This kind of loss is also common when loved ones have dementia or a mental health disorder, because you are grieving for the person you knew, the bond you had.

"You can't cope with something unless you know what it is, so giving it a name helps people deal with the stress of it," Dr. Boss told me. Over the years, she's worked with prisoners of war, families coping with Alzheimer's, and with individual patients in her practice. At eighty-seven years old, she's experienced her share of grief as well, losing siblings, parents, close friends, and, more recently, her husband.

Jackie's close friends experienced ambiguous loss, just as I did. For years, they tried to help her, and they mourned the Jackie they knew when she was not her addiction.

"The thing with this disease is that no one is at fault," says Jackie's close friend Mike, who asked me not to use his last name. He met Jackie in Alcoholics Anonymous and served as a kind of father figure to her over the course of many years. He knew, just as we did, that as maddening as her actions might be, she wasn't intentionally causing harm. "There are all sorts of diseases, and it's the same with this. No one can explain why it happens. Maybe God could explain it."

My parents, my sisters, and I became close with Mike and his wife Grainne, who was Jackie's AA sponsor, over the years. They became her New York family, her closest friends. They went to weekly dinners together, day trips to Coney Island, and overnight trips upstate. They picked up groceries for each other, spent holidays and birthdays together. They knew each other's secrets, and deepest fears. Since she died, they've helped me understand who she was in AA meetings, and what she meant to them and to others in the program.

"Jackie made an impression on me right away," Grainne told me about the first time she saw my sister at a meeting. "She spoke about what was going on with her and I just remember thinking that I wanted to help her. She was very intelligent, and she had so much information about everything. If anyone had a question, she always had an answer. I loved talking to her about music and art and style."

Mike, a lifelong New Yorker born and raised in Queens, says that the first time he met my Texas-bred sister, she hugged him.

"I just thought, gee, isn't that sweet," he says. "I loved her. She really pursued her career and went to school to be an aesthetician, but this lousy, stinking alcohol always gets in the way. It's a real terrible disease."

Their relationship with Jackie, like mine, was at times tumultuous. They took both Jackie and Niall to detoxes, tried their best to help them both, and traveled with them to small towns upstate or to the beach when they were sober. But loving an alcoholic is an exercise in patience and acceptance.

"I felt so bad because I thought that maybe I didn't do enough, but there is nothing I could have done," Grainne, who spoke to my sister nearly every day, says of Jackie's death. "I lost my sister, too, and it's like losing your arm."

Jackie's best friend Amelia told me that she first noticed my sister at an AA meeting "because her hair was very red. It looked glamorous on her, but on me I would look like a troll."

Jackie was the maid of honor at Amelia's wedding, and she became like an aunt to Amelia's son. They'd eat at Donovan's Pub or the Copper Kettle in Queens, shop at thrift stores, or spend the day in Far Rockaway. When they went to AA meetings together, they each had their favorite seat, right next to each other. Amelia says Jackie loved going to the Queens County Farm to feed the animals, something I never knew she did.

There's a photo of Jackie that Amelia, Mike, and Grainne have all shared on Facebook that shows my sister standing in front of an ornate, bright red restaurant door, which is the same shade as her lipstick. She's wearing a strapless fuchsia minidress, dark, oversized cat-eye sunglasses, and holding a black purse with fringe. Her waist-length, vibrant red hair hangs over her pale shoulder in a low ponytail. There is nothing timid or meek about this picture, but for those of us who knew Jackie, the swirl of color and style can't mask her struggles.

"When speaking to her you would never think she was anxious, but then she would tell me she was up at two in the morning having a panic attack, and she'd go to work the next morning. To me, that sounds maddening," Amelia says. She told me she still has a hard time wrapping her head around the events in Colorado that led to Jackie's death. "If I knew this was going to happen, I would have set fire to their car before they left New York," she says.

Amelia says that with alcohol dependency, no one can be completely sure this won't happen to them. It's not as if Jackie were weaker than others who manage to stay sober for the rest of their lives.

"You can stop and have everything you want," Amelia says of sobriety. "It doesn't have to be this way. That doesn't mean life will get amazing overnight, but you take steps toward what you really want and find other ways to manage your feelings, or it will destroy your life. I really don't think Jackie knew what was coming."

It is estimated that 95,000 people in America die from alcohol-related causes annually. That's about 260 people each day. Worldwide, the number is three million a year. And there are millions of us who love them, or loved them, each in our own ways.

I'm not sure if it would have made it any easier to understand and live with my sister's alcoholism if I had heard about ambiguous loss years earlier, but now it helps me make sense of the conflicting emotions I felt when my sister was still alive, the times I would catch myself imagining getting "the call," telling me she had, in fact, died. The strange moments I would find myself tearing up while envisioning her funeral, and then feeling horribly guilty, not knowing where that morbid impulse came from. The times I felt a deep sadness that I couldn't place, when really it was because my baby sister was gone. Alive, but not the same. Here, but unreachable.

How do you summarize years of anger, confusion, and fear. It's tough to distill the complexities of my relationship with my sister Jackie. The years it took to finally even comprehend the seriousness of her addictions, and the struggle to understand why she couldn't "just quit." She spent her early twenties in and out of rehabs, but I kept thinking, *She's young. Eventually she'll "get it together."* But as soon as things seemed to get better, they always got worse. I would get Facebook messages from people I had never met, telling me they heard my sister was sleeping on a park bench, or that she'd somehow turned up in Miami with no wallet or cell phone. She lost so many phones over the years that I had to change her contact information to "JackieUseThis" or "Jackie 2019" and then, finally, "Jackie2020." I could have updated her number each time, but I guess I grew weary. It was less effort to let the numbers pile up. Our last text thread is saved under "Jackie2020." The final texts, sent in February 2021, were from Jackie, checking in on me during the Texas winter storm that turned the entire, unprepared state into a block of ice. She wanted to see if I was okay. I told her that I was. We spoke on the phone once more after that, but I could hear a subtle shift in her tone, and I knew she'd started drinking again, after nearly a year of sobriety. It just took one sip to push her back into that horrible cycle. By that time, my senses were acutely aware of any changes in her voice. On that call, I said goodbye quickly, not because I was angry with her, as I had been so many times in the past. I had learned enough about addiction by then not to be angry. I was just worn out, I felt horrible for her, and I understood that there was nothing I could say, besides "I love you."

I didn't realize it would be the last time I would hear her voice, one that is still so clear in my mind. I hold onto that sweet voice, playing it like a rare recording whenever I miss her. I'm afraid that, one day, I'll lose the ability to conjure her voice, or my mother's voice. I guess if that happens, I can listen to the few messages I've saved, as a reminder. It takes courage to play those voicemails, though. I know listening to them will temporarily destroy me, so I rarely, if ever, do it.

Here's a text exchange, from February 10, 2021:

> **Jackie:** I spoke on a Zoom meeting today.
>
> My topic was resilience and strength.
>
> **Me:** How did it feel?
>
> **Jackie:** Good. I cried a bit. They were good tears though because I know a lot of people are struggling.
>
> Some people fight a disease they can't win.
>
> I did for many years
>
> **Me:** 🖤

I was so proud of Jackie in those moments, and I also felt so much sadness for what she had to endure. Why her? She wasn't some monster. She was a kind, sweet human being who didn't deserve any of this. By that time, so many years in, I could imagine how difficult it must have been for her to wake up each morning and not drink, to get through another day and not let her addiction claw through her resolve. In those moments, I would tell my sister how proud of her I was. We all would. She had all the love and encouragement in the world. Sometimes though, that just isn't enough. Nothing is.

"I was proud of her when she finally acknowledged her illness," my dad told me when I asked what it was like for him and my mom, watching a daughter struggle with substance abuse. "She always told me, 'I don't want this life. I wish I could be like my sisters and go out and have fun and then go home. But I can't.' She went to meetings and spoke, she sponsored other alcoholics, and I was proud of her because she really did try. She worked her program and did what she could do, but it was a long journey for nineteen years."

Three weeks after Jackie sent me those final texts, almost two decades into her struggle, she would be found dead in that Colorado motel room. The exact date will probably always be unknown, which is a mystery that I imagine many loved ones of addicts and alcoholics live with as well, since so many die alone, and an autopsy can often only provide a guess. I would later attempt to solve that mystery, but my detective skills have limits. What does not have limits is my imagination. I may never stop picturing that motel room in Colorado. I haven't seen it and I definitely don't plan on visiting, but an image of it is forever burned into my brain. It's inky blue and dimly lit, maybe as a subconscious survival tactic to keep me from seeing too much. Nearly every time I pass a roadside motel, that image materializes. I try to look away, and shut it out.

Jackie and I didn't live in the same state for a long time, since I left Texas for California at eighteen years old. I wasn't confronted with the reality of what was happening to her, as my parents and younger sisters were. I could call Jackie when I wanted to, or see her during a holiday. She was better at hiding things then. I would hear the heartbreak in my parents' voices when they told me she'd gone missing, or checked into treatment again, usually after they begged her to. It nearly broke them, which is where most of my early anger came from. *How could she do this to Mom and Dad, two wonderful people who loved her and supported her no matter what? Why was she so selfish? What was wrong with her?* It took a long time for me to come to terms with the fact that Jackie wasn't *doing* anything to my parents. She was selfish when she was using, but she was tortured, too, in ways we couldn't comprehend.

My dad said that, eventually, he and my mom learned some coping skills; otherwise, the relationship would have been unbearable. They stopped enabling her, by not paying a bill or not sending rent money if she asked. "It's one of the hardest things to do, because you want to give things to your child, but we couldn't, and we realized that," he says. "I learned that if I was going to stay sane, I had to have boundaries with my own child to go on."

Ambiguous loss can stem from loving an addict, and it can also come from things like a painful breakup, an estrangement, or, in the case of my friend Alisa, a kidnapping. During the first year he was held captive in Pakistan, she says, if anyone asked her about her dad she would "literally have to lean on something. My breathing got labored and I couldn't talk about it. Now I can talk about it all day long." She says, at first, there was an "overwhelming physical response" that she couldn't control.

Alisa had no words to describe what she was feeling until she heard about ambiguous loss. "I didn't even know about calling it grief," she said. "I just remember feeling the deepest sadness I'd ever experienced. I couldn't even describe it in words. I didn't want to reach out to friends because I wouldn't even know what to say." For her, this kind of grief, not knowing whether her father was alive or dead, and feeling like she had no way to express it, was "an incredibly lonely experience."

There are no ceremonies and rituals to mark this kind of loss, because it's ongoing. Throughout 2020, there was a universal sense of dread, and not just about the virus that we feared. We were prohibited from having our usual ceremonies, like funerals or wakes or homegoings. We lost loved ones, daily routines, and our most basic sense of security. Simply walking past a neighbor felt dangerous. Playgrounds were wrapped in caution tape. Everything around us was the same, but not.

That's how my relationship with Jackie felt so much of the time: the same, but not. Even so, no matter how strained our relationship would get, our shared history, our bond as sisters, could never be erased. There were plenty of times over the years that I wished I could erase it, though. Times I wanted nothing more to do with her. I was done (again), I was never speaking to her (again). I felt this way the week our mom was home in hospice care, because Jackie was in such bad shape she couldn't even fly out to help, or be with our mother in her final days.

"I'm done with her. I hate her," I said to my dad after a heated phone call with Jackie that week. "I mean it this time—I'm never speaking to her again."

Maybe I meant it in the moment, but those grand proclamations never lasted. I would always talk to her again. When we got the text that she was walking up to the door during that hospice week, I became tense, a coiled spring ready to snap. The second I saw her, the springs unraveled like a kite string. Unlike that morning in the streets of Manhattan, I did run to her and hug her. She was thin, distracted, and detached. I held her tight and didn't care if she couldn't give me the love I craved from her at that moment. I knew, somewhere deep down in her pain, that she loved me, too. No matter what state she was in, Jackie was also being forced to say goodbye to her own mother. Like so many things in our past, we would forever be bonded in that.

Detach with love.

I first heard this phrase in a dusty basement of a brownstone in the West Village. After months of anxiety and spiraling, I had found my way, at last, to an Al-Anon meeting. Founded in 1951, Al-Anon is a recovery and support group for family and friends of alcoholics. I went there out of desperation, knowing that what I was doing was not working. My anxiety, codependency, and enabling (insert any number of faulty coping mechanisms here) wasn't healthy, for me or my sister. My parents had gone to Al-Anon meetings, and it helped them, too. If you love someone deeply, it's impossible to stand aside and watch them destroy their life. It tears you apart. The harder you try to fix things, the more helpless you feel, and then you blame them for putting you in that position. I was gutted and worn down, and, looking back, getting close to a breakdown myself. I didn't have a therapist, and I needed help.

At the Al-Anon meeting, people shared their stories of pain or loss. They talked about spouses, siblings, friends, and parents. One woman talked about her financial woes, so I'm pretty sure she was using Al-Anon as a free therapy session. Eventually, I got the courage to raise my hand. I cried, and talked about Jackie. I emptied myself out to a circle of strangers. One guy, who looked to be in his thirties, told stories about his wife, who was back in rehab. An older woman talked about her husband who had struggled for years, and who couldn't keep a job, leaving her to carry the financial burden. None of these people told me how to "fix" it. They didn't say it would all work out. They told me to detach with love. It was the only way to survive, they said. Some phrases can take a while to truly click into your brain. You might nod in recognition, but their full meaning might need to marinate for weeks or months, until you finally absorb it. Not this, though. *Detach with love* was an immediate "aha" moment for me. A hallelujah. It made so much sense. Just because I immediately grasped the meaning deep in my bones, though, doesn't mean it made everything immediately better.

For the next fourteen years, I detached with love whenever it was necessary. That might mean I wouldn't always answer the phone if I knew Jackie was drinking and possibly belligerent, or it might mean that, if I did answer and hear that familiar slowing of her speech, I would gently tell her I loved her, but to please get help and call me when she was sober. It allows you to step back, without guilt or anger. It gives you permission to focus on your own life, instead of allowing their life to drive yours into the ground. It's not always easy to detach, though. My parents never stopped answering Jackie's calls, even though my dad told me, "If she was drinking, I could not handle being around her in that condition. That was a boundary she and I had."

When she was in the hospital in New York once after a bad relapse, I flew out from California to sit by her side. I didn't have kids yet, as my other sisters did, and my dad was caring for my mom during a particularly rough stretch of chemo, so off I went. I couldn't detach completely, not when my baby sister was alone, fragile, and being questioned by hospital psychiatrists about the color of her hair.

Jackie told me she wanted me to stay in the room while the psych team talked to her, and I remember the protective anger that reared up inside me when the lead psychiatrist in her white coat asked my sister, "So, tell me about your red hair." I had been puzzled by Jackie's red hair for years. My mom was always begging me to tell Jackie to go back to her natural brown curls, as if my words would have made a difference. We were all confused by her hair, but how dare this rude, horrible woman question my sister's choice of hair dye. Where did she get her medical degree—clown school?

Jackie, always so gloriously deadpan even in her worst moments, replied, "I don't know, I just like it. Tell me about *your* hair color."

The psychiatrist moved on to a new topic after that.

Just as she always did, Jackie made it out of that hospital and back into sobriety again, for a time. No psychiatrist was going to make her doubt her choice of hair color, or question something that made her feel good about herself. After that day in the hospital, I respected her maroon- or ruby- or copper-colored tresses just a little bit more. I like to imagine that through those colors, she was saying screw you to a world that didn't understand her.

"Oh my gosh, her style," Grainne told me when I brought up my sister's fiery hair. "I was mesmerized by her style. She had such a great attention to detail, and I always felt proud to be with her."

I worried about Jackie in New York in the early days of 2020, as the pandemic hit. During the previous two years, she'd been heading down a dangerous path of drinking to the point that ambulances would take her to detox at least every few weeks. If the hospital had an available detox bed, Jackie would be supervised and safely weaned off alcohol and drugs for a few days, unless she decided to walk out on her own, which she often did. The hope was that after safely detoxing, she would check into a rehab that was covered by Medicaid, usually somewhere upstate. After rehab she might live in a sober living house for a while, and then, after finding another new job, into her own apartment. Thinking of her wandering out of detox as a dangerous pandemic swept across the country had me panicked. In those early days of Lysoling our groceries and locking ourselves away like petrified moles, the fear that a virus could kill my sister was real. If anyone died during that time, our collective, immediate thought was usually, "I'll bet it was Covid." If they were hit by a bus right in front of our eyes, we wondered if it was Covid. They could ingest a gallon of arsenic, and we would assume it was not just the poison, but the poison *plus* Covid. I wasn't sure that Jackie, in a compromised state, would remember to wear a mask. I was afraid her immune system wouldn't be able to handle such an unpredictable illness if she did get sick.

One sense of relief I had during that time was that my sister got sober and was doing amazingly well. She sounded healthy and upbeat. She was holding a steady job. During the summer of 2020, she finally left Queens with Niall and moved to Colorado, a place they'd been talking about for years. She didn't have a new job yet, but she had her cat, and her daily walks and jogs, surrounded by mountains. She was cooking and watching movies. We were talking nearly every week. Actually talking. I knew enough to understand that relapses could always happen, and that they were part of recovery, but I allowed myself to have some hope that, maybe this time, she could make it. If she didn't, she would start again. No matter how many times you've been through the ups and downs, it's hard to doubt an addict when you love them. Despite the odds, hope is crucial. I cherish the relationship I had with Jackie during the last year of her life. I'm grateful we were on good terms, loving terms, at the end.

Jackie never met my son Cole, even though he was three years old when she died. For the first two years of his life she wasn't in any shape to visit, and when she did come to Houston to see my mom during hospice, Cole was asleep upstairs. In 2020, she would constantly talk about visiting, telling me how excited she was to meet him. She loved kids. She wanted kids of her own, but it never happened. She wanted so badly to see all her nieces and nephews. Because of the pandemic, we were all skittish about travel. Simple visits weren't so simple anymore. I finally told Jackie to just come, to just get in the car and drive. We were getting so close to a visit. But, mainly because of the pandemic, we kept pushing it off. We were trying to be responsible, at a time when no one in the world knew what to do. How I wish we hadn't put that visit off.

In February 2021, my sister started drinking again. The last week of that month she went missing, and even my dad hadn't heard from her, which was odd, since he was the person she always reached out to, no matter what. My mom and my sisters and I tended to let our emotions lead in our interactions with Jackie, but my dad always stayed calm and rational, which I think allowed her to confide in him. Now, though, she wasn't responding to him, but we assumed this would eventually follow the familiar plot of detox, rehab, sobriety, again. After two days, the police finally located her in that motel. We waited for the next call, which would hopefully be from Jackie, calling from yet another new cell number, assuring us that she was getting help, again.

> Hey Deanie, it's Jackie. Here's my new number
> if you need it.

That call never came.

Why did the police wait an entire day to tell us Jackie had died, after they found her? If Jackie had been a young mother, an upstanding citizen in the community, Miss Colorado, or president of a corporation, would they have called right away? Was it because she was "just" another drunk to them? A throwaway person, a name on a page? Addicts and alcoholics are all so much more than this. They're the people we love, the ones we knew, the siblings or parents or cousins or friends we ache for each day, whether they're here with us or not. To the people who find them, though, sometimes they are just a name on a page. Paperwork they need to fill out before moving on to the next case.

For a few days, like an amateur Sherlock Holmes, I investigated. I talked to friends of my sister who had actually heard from her during those final days, and they led me down a rabbit hole of odd texts and strange numbers and screenshots and foul play conspiracies. Maybe someone put pills in Jackie's drinks, or maybe she overdosed and this person fled, leaving her alone in that room. One theory was that she'd been kidnapped and then abandoned in the motel. Someone sent me a Colorado number, which Jackie had texted to them late one night, as if to say, these are the people I'm with, someone may need this. After several hours I got the courage to dial the number.

A woman answered.

"Hi. Who is this?" I asked.

"Tiffany. Who's this?"

I explained to this stranger, Tiffany, that I was Jackie's sister, that her number was in my sister's phone, and that I wanted to know what happened.

"I saw your sister stumbling in the street, so we brought her back to our hotel and let her shower. I gave her some food, but she was in pretty bad shape. I don't think she even knew where she was."

"Do you know what happened to her? Were there any drugs? Anything you can tell me?"

Remember, I said *amateur* Sherlock Holmes. As if Tiffany would tell a stranger on the phone that she had a hotel room full of cocaine and Klonopin.

"Is she okay?" Tiffany asked.

"She's dead," I said, my voice shaking.

"I don't know what happened. She was okay when we left her. Is she okay now?" Tiffany asked again.

"She's dead," I repeated.

"Huh?"

"My sister is fucking dead, and I need to know what happened to her!"

I hated hearing these words. I hated saying them. What else was there, though? Tiffany was clearly not all there. I couldn't change or erase or rewind what had happened. I just wanted an answer, one that an autopsy, which took two months to complete, couldn't give me. Apparently, Tiffany didn't have answers, either, or if she did, she wasn't talking.

Tiffany did seem genuinely shocked when she finally mumbled some words, which were probably "I'm sorry" or "Oh, my god" or "Oh, shit." I can't remember exactly what she said. When we hung up, I called the detective in Colorado and left another message, this time giving him Tiffany's number and telling him he might want to question her. But I knew. It wasn't a boogeyman or a crazed drug dealer or

Tiffany who killed my sister. It was years of substance abuse, and one relapse. It's hard to grasp that at just forty years old, a drink can lead to the end of your life. There is no mystery in that. There's just the reality that, like millions of others who suffer through this, Jackie, my sister, is gone.

Is one form of loss tougher to cope with than another? Grief is grief, whether it is sudden and shocking, or a long road with an inevitable end point. I got to say goodbye to my mom for days as she lay in hospice, but I didn't get that with my sister. I hadn't seen her in over two years when she died, but I have a lifetime of memories with her, good and bad. I also have our final year, when she was healthy and we would talk often, and I would hear her sweet laugh. There was nothing anyone could have done, except Jackie herself. But it's still not her fault. That might be tough to understand if you believe that addicts and alcoholics have a "choice" to use or not to use. If only it were that simple. I know for a fact that my sister wished it were that simple. What if we had defied our pandemic fears and decided to see each other? Would that have made her think twice about drinking again? If she had chosen to call one of us from that motel, would our pleas and our love have saved her? The answers, and the questions, are irrelevant. The grief, the pain, is not.

In a perfect world, we would have had the funeral as soon as possible, but it took about a week to have my sister transferred from Colorado back home to Texas. Once again, we faced the paperwork, the phone calls, the frustration, and waiting in the midst of so much emotional agony. When she was finally in Houston, in the care of Uncle Lev, who had handled our mom's funeral not so long before, we had a choice. We could go to the funeral home for a viewing, to say goodbye, or not. In Jewish tradition, there is typically not a viewing, so this wasn't something we were used to doing. Add to that the fact that it's also tradition not to embalm the body, which I understand is a lot to hear, but this was in our minds, it was part of our fear, as we drove to the funeral home. In the car with my father, Amy, my brother-in-law Mike, and Kathryn, I was silent. All I could do was stare out the window and breathe, in an attempt to keep my anxiety at a manageable level. We had so many hours and days to say goodbye to our mom, but we hadn't seen Jackie in so long. Was it wrong not to see her? Would it traumatize us if we did? What was the best choice? Morally, it had nothing to do with "right" or "wrong." It had to do with what we could handle, and what we each needed in order to say goodbye.

The funeral home was decorated with antiques. A few tattered magazines were spread across a table for people to read, if they were curious about things like old *Southern Living* recipes from 2015. We quietly discussed whether or not we should go in and see her. None of us were sure. Then Lev came into the waiting room.

"Hi, everyone. You can see her now, if you're ready."

Without any discussion, we gripped each other's hands and headed to the large double doors leading into the sanctuary room, where Jackie lay in her casket. We didn't want our dad doing this alone. And, despite our fear, we wanted, needed, to see her.

Seconds after we walked into the silent, high-ceilinged room and could see Jackie, Kathryn fell to the floor. Our dad let out a sigh so deep, it looked like he might faint. He found the courage to walk right up to his little girl, kiss her forehead, and say, "I love you my little brown bean," which was the nickname he'd called her since childhood, because of her dark brown curly hair. His love for her, his ability to face this, helped me move closer. I touched her hand, which was, unlike my mom's had been, ice cold. I kissed her forehead, also cold. We told her how much we loved her, how sorry we were that she had to endure so many years of struggle, ending like this, in this lonely room so heavy with loss. I can't remember the paintings on the wall, or whether or not there were vases or candles or color of any kind. I do remember the quiet, broken up by a sigh or a sob. An occasional whisper of "I can't believe this is real." There was her bright red hair, though, which I touched, one last time. After so many years of questioning why she chose such a brazen color, in that moment, she would not have seemed like my sister, the Jackie I knew, without it.

It could have been ten minutes or twenty, maybe an hour, when we decided it was time to leave. The next struggle, for my dad at least, was deciding whether or not to bury Jackie with Niall's wedding band, as he'd requested. In traditional Judaism, you're not *supposed* to be buried with any possessions, but my sisters and I were all for Jackie having the ring. My mom got her wig, after all. People have been buried with Ferraris (true story) and guitars, so a small wedding band seemed pretty harmless.

To ease my dad's guilt, I asked Lev if he buried other Jewish people with possessions.

"You should see some of the things I'm asked to put in caskets," Lev mercifully said. "Astros jackets, beer cans, tennis balls, casino chips, dice, small bottles of the deceased's favorite type of alcohol, rocks, beach sand, ping-pong balls . . ."

It was decided. The ring would remain with Jackie. We thanked Lev, again, and headed out to the car, knowing that whatever energy we had left needed to be saved for the funeral, where a small group of family members would gather around, wearing masks. As much as we dreaded it, we knew we were lucky to have that ritual, since, just one year before, so many people were not allowed to stand together around a loved one's grave. This was on my mind the day of the funeral, when I saw strangers setting up a camera, so Jackie's closest friends, her New York family, her AA "parents" Mike and Grainne, her best friend Amelia, her husband Niall, who said goodbye to her at the Colorado funeral home before she was transferred, could watch via Zoom.

None of this is easy. Not funerals or lack of funerals or saying goodbye. Viewings, decisions, long car rides where you're just trying to focus on each breath, on the trees outside, on anything to keep you grounded.

Then there is also the fact that loving an addict and facing ambiguous loss can be incredibly lonely. It can tear you apart, if you let it. It's a struggle, whether they are here or not. People sometimes say, "She's not suffering anymore." They say she's with our mom, our grandparents, all the beloved cats she had over the years. I hope all of this is true. I want her here, though, sober and thriving and leaving me voicemails that say, "Hey, Deanie . . ." I will want that forever. You can yearn for an alternate reality, but also accept what happened. I don't yearn for that alternate reality constantly. I live side by side with the loss. But I can't pretend that, every now and then, instead of telling myself she's not suffering anymore, I just want her back.

My sister was so much more than her disease, and that's what I carry with me.

I hold onto that, and to Jackie's affection and empathy, her passion for animals and her love of campy horror and David Bowie's music. Her deep kindness, her bone-dry sense of humor, and—maybe most of all—her puzzling, ever-changing, beautiful burgundy hair.

Chapter 8
J'aime Mon Chien

When my sisters and I had all moved out of the house, my parents adopted a pug named Brodie. He was the runt of the litter, and they were obsessed with this precious, snorting ball of love. He was basically their first grandchild. During the Brodie era, one day when my mom was feeling sorry for herself because her daughters weren't reproducing fast enough, or at all, she said, in the most perfect example of passive-aggressive Southern Speak I can think of, "I guess I'll die before I have any grandchildren." For several years, Brodie was all she had, as far as grandkids go.

My mom had pillows with pugs embroidered on them. Little paintings of pugs still hang around the house. When Brodie died at just six years old, my parents were crushed. He *was* the runt, but still. Nothing prepares you. They swore they would never get another dog, and they stuck by that vow. Now my dad is taking care of a seventeen-year-old Hemingway cat named Kathryn that once belonged to Jackie. Over the years, Jackie named a cat after each of her sisters. There was a Dina and an Amy at some point, but, unlike Kathryn, our feline counterparts weren't long for this world. Even though she is between 84 and 112 in human years (depending on which state-of-the-art cat age calculator you use) and she has health issues, my dad cannot bring himself to put Kathryn the cat down. He drives across town to pick up her medication, and he won't spend more than two days away from her. Maybe I'm projecting, but I think that after so much loss in such a short time, he just can't bear to lose anyone else—human or feline.

It just takes a quick stroll through any pet store on earth to see how much we humans love our animals. We buy them hoodies, hats, boots, toys, fancy treats, bows, and organic cookies. Thanks to Martha Stewart, there are CBD products for pets, and she just loves PrettyLitter, which is cat litter made with some sort of absorbent crystals. We shower our animals with adoration and call them "fur babies." Many pets have a damn good gig, and when we lose them, those fancy treats and dog booties remind us that they're gone. People are often embarrassed to mourn pets the way we mourn people. Maybe that needs to change. In some places, it already is changing.

If you travel north of Portland to Clatskanie, Oregon, you can visit the Great Vow Zen Monastery. At this monastery you'll find a Pacific Northwest garden, lush with moss, cedar trees, big leaf maples, trillium, salmonberry, and ferns. Scattered throughout this garden, among the vegetation, you'll see small stone statues, representing the Japanese Buddhist guardian deity Jizo. Eyes closed in peaceful repose, Jizo protects women, children, and travelers, and helps ease the pain of parents who are grieving for a child. In this garden, and in Jizo gardens around the world, the bereaved can place and dedicate a statue to the specific person they lost, decorating the statue with mementos like jewelry or beads, and clothing them in traditional bright red knit caps and bibs. Over time, any statue that's placed in the garden at Great Vow will become covered with thick green moss.

According to the monastery's co-abbot Jan Chozen Bays, scattered around the Jizo garden in Clatskanie, you'll also find a handful of statues commemorating a beloved cat or dog.

"For many people, a pet is their child," she says. "I want everybody to feel included. We can't weigh a person's grief. You can't predict a person's grief. We can't judge a person's grief. So I think it's really important to be as inclusive as possible."

If you still doubt that the death of animals has less of an impact than the loss of a person, just ask Dolly Parton. Her 1974 song "Cracker Jack" is all about a beloved rescue pup she found by the riverbank in rural Appalachia as a kid. She forged a deep and lasting bond with Cracker Jack, and you can hear the love and longing in her sweet voice when she sings about him—accompanied by her closer-to-God blond hair and her acoustic guitar, of course. Also ask Chris Stapleton, Luke Bryan, Carrie Underwood, or Hank Williams. If you think most country songs are about breakups, bottles of booze, and big old trucks, just google COUNTRY SONGS ABOUT DOGS and a slew of odes will appear. In Stapleton's tune "Maggie's Song," he sings, definitively, that dogs have souls. Thanks to his beloved Maggie, there is not a doubt in his mind.

Stapleton and Dolly Parton understand what most pet lovers feel: A dog is not "just" a dog. And sometimes, a pet can mean as much as a parent. Have you seen movies or read books like *Call of the Wild*, *Old Yeller*, or the cruelest of all children's required reading materials, *Where the Red Fern Grows*? They tear you up inside. Gut you. Temporarily plunge you into a grief so agonizing, it feels like you may never recover until someone hands you a cookie. These stories are told for a reason. Connections with animals tap into our humanity. As my grandmother often said, you can't trust someone who doesn't like animals. Unless you're highly allergic or have had scary, life-threatening experiences. In those cases, you get a pass.

We expect to outlive our pets, but that doesn't mean we're prepared for the moment they leave us. I lost cats and dogs throughout childhood, which I admit did not remotely compare to losing a family member or friend. But the moment I brought home my own puppy, Indy, and I looked into his soulful green eyes, I knew a horrible day would come, eventually, when we would lose him. This dog hugs me. Actually *hugs* me. All he wants is affection, and the occasional treat. He is a world-class cuddler and when he chases a butterfly, forget it. Every time I see him do this, my heart explodes with love.

When he got a stinger in his paw a week after we brought him home, I grabbed a magnifying glass and tweezers and sat on the floor with him for half an hour, determined to end his pain. Imagining a larger, meaner dog or coyote harming him terrifies me. When we first brought him home and he was still small, I would stand guard whenever he ran around outside, in case a ravenous owl decided to swoop down and grab some twelve-pound prey. And don't get me started on stories of dogs who die from drinking lake water full of poisonous blue-green algae. The point is, our love for our animals runs deep (and also, apparently, makes us paranoid). That love doesn't evaporate when a pet dies. It stays with us, and reminds us that our animals have a more profound impact on our lives than we may realize.

When I spoke to Chozen, the abbot from Great Vow, she brought up the many ways that pets enrich our lives. They can improve our mental and physical well-being, give us a purpose, put things in perspective. They comfort the sick and protect the young. Parents of older children who have left home can sometimes become incredibly attached to their pets.

"Grief is grief," says Kaleel Sakakeeny, a pet loss and bereavement counselor and CEO of Animal Talks, a Boston-based nonprofit that helps people navigate the grief of a pet. For him, there is no difference between the feelings experienced when you lose a pet or a person. He says that he's heard more people talking about grief in the last few years than he has in his entire lifetime, largely due to the pandemic. Those conversations are about all kinds of loss, and it's allowing people to accept grief as a part of life, and removing the shame of expressing your pain over the death of a person or a pet.

"People are becoming aware that grief and love are conjoined emotions," he says. Sakakeeny brings up the intense bonds we witness between people and their pets during natural disasters like Hurricane Katrina, or during the 2022 war in Ukraine as an example of that love.

"You see the sacrifices people are willing to make to stay with animals, or you see seniors who lost everything and the last thing they need is to lose their animal companion. Descartes really screwed us up by talking about animals being robots," he says, referring to the seventeenth-century French philosopher René Descartes, who declared that animals were machines, without thought or consciousness. Clearly Descartes was either a serial killer or he just never came into close contact with a kitten, rabbit, bird, pig, cow, horse, or dog (*un chien* to him).

Sakakeeny says it's common for people to come to him with feelings of guilt or embarrassment because of the intensity of their emotions over losing a pet. People will often say things like, "I cried harder when my dog died than when my mom died. What is wrong with me?" He says that grieving the loss of a pet can allow us to unleash pent-up emotions about other losses, like the loss of a parent. Our human relationships are often complex, but with animals it's usually so pure, and there isn't much there to block our outpouring of emotion, like bitter feuds or grudges that might complicate our grief. For example, a pet won't gamble away your life savings or tarnish the family name by engaging in insider trading.

"The death of a pet can become a gateway to incredibly intense therapy," Sakakeeny says.

So pets are not "just" pets. And if you think they are, you might be doing the pet thing wrong. Or else you're a serial killer, like Descartes.

For some of us, losing a pet might be the first time we learn about death or experience grief. A 2020 study by researchers at Massachusetts General Hospital found that, for children, loss of a pet can trigger prolonged distress and even depression. Before we had Indy, my son Cole got very attached to the toads, dragonflies, and crickets in our yard. Maybe this is because he's an only child and he badly needed a companion, or maybe he's just a massive lover of all creatures great and small. Perhaps he'll grow up to become a world-renowned herpetologist. He cried when I told him he couldn't bring a toad he'd named Adrienne inside to sleep in his bed with him. He was later startled when, one bright morning, we walked down the driveway and found a large, flattened toad right there on the concrete. It was possible that it was one of the "friends" he had been chasing the night before, or even, God forbid, Adrienne. I braced for his reaction.

"Mommy, what happened? It died?"

"Yes, honey. I'm sorry."

"Why did it die?"

It didn't seem like a smart move to admit that his dad or I probably ran over Adrienne or one of his toad buddies with our car, so I did what most parents do when they have no clue what to say. I deflected.

"Do you want to say goodbye to the toad?"

Cole did want to say something to the toad. He said he was sorry he died, he loved him, and goodbye. The bonds he had with that toad are not nearly as strong as the connection he has with our dog Indy, who is basically Cole's brother. He wasn't devastated by the sight of the dead toad, but he was sad and confused, as kids are at that age when the subject of death comes up. I often talk about my mom and sister to Cole, even though he doesn't have a memory of either one of them, not that I can tell. When he asks where Cici and Jackie are, I say they died but they're here with us and they love him very much. It's difficult to talk to my son about death, whether it's a toad or his grandmother. That might sound ridiculous, but children are not born with a sense of what grief or death actually means, and it's up to us to teach them, but it's not the simplest thing to "teach." So pets and animals often become the first experiences they have with loss as they attempt to learn what this daunting concept of death even means. In that sense, animals are incredibly important when it comes to learning about grief. Those are not throw-away connections. They enable us to understand, or attempt to understand, the mysteries of our own existence.

When people come to Sakakeeny in distress about their pets, he says his main job is to listen, not to make the pain go away. "Our medical model is to 'fix' things, to return people to normal, but there is no normal anymore," he says of grief, whether it's over a pet or a parent. He says that people often ask him things like this: Is their pet in heaven or will they be reunited with their pet one day? Their belief system is rocked, and they want answers.

"I say, 'What do you *want* to believe in?' And that's what guides you," he says. When they answer that question, "It then becomes a new definition of who they are. What you yearn to believe in is the deeper truth."

I yearn to believe that my mom is hanging out with her pug Brodie, right next to Jackie who is surrounded by the fifteen animals she adopted over the years, beside my grand-mother Mamaw, who is with her cat Sunny. Is that rational? Not at all. Does it help? Absolutely.

"You feel such emptiness when they're gone," says Mari-lyn Sherwin, a retiree in Florida who also happens to be my husband's aunt. Marilyn's defining characteristic among everyone who knows her is her connection with her animals. Throughout her adult life, she's always had dogs, horses, and cats, and these animals are, without a doubt, family to her.

Marilyn says she was actually scared of dogs as a little girl, but when her grandparents gave her a poodle, everything changed. "She was my best friend," Marilyn says. "Later I switched to German shepherds. They just seemed like a better fit for me."

She named her first German shepherd Veruschka, after the famous 1960s model. When Veruschka was hit by a car at just three years old, Marilyn was devastated. She asked her brother-in-law to take the nearly eighty-pound dog to the vet, and then to get her cremated, so she could keep Veruschka's ashes. Marilyn bought an ornate box and gave it to her brother-in-law when it was time to pick up Veruschka's remains. As he poured the ashes in, he realized that Marilyn hadn't gotten a large enough box, so he did what he believed to be the humane thing. He put as many ashes into the box as he could, and threw away the rest.

Marilyn kept that ornate box in her home for years before she learned the truth. At a family gathering, she overheard her brother-in-law telling the story of Veruschka, but adding that the box hadn't been big enough, so he fit as much of Veruschka in as he could. For years, Marilyn had been living with half a dog.

"I was like, Why did you ever have to tell the truth?" she says.

Now, when a pet dies she handles the arrangements herself, and that includes burying her horse "G" with a tombstone that reads G Marilyn Sherwin.

"When I go visit her, it's like I'm buried there," Marilyn says. "I guess I should have thought of that."

Like many pet owners, Marilyn keeps mementos of her animals, and even talks to them, via photos or their urns. Now she has their ashes placed in little (but not *too* little) wooden boxes imprinted with a clay mold of their paw print and their name.

"It's just something more of them," she says. "I could never totally part with my animals. I never had kids, and even my horses are so much a part of me. The only time I'm at peace with myself is when I'm with my animals. They're never judging you. They just appreciate you for you."

Marilyn says that when a pet dies, it's never an easy decision to get a new dog or cat. It took a year after her last German shepherd, Arabella, died before she was remotely ready to think about a new animal. Now, she has Anna, who, she says, looks oddly like Arabella. "She has the same markings and everything," Marilyn says.

Sometimes, getting a new pet is the best way to process your loss.

Jake, a physician in California who asked me not to use his real name, told me that his advice to anyone who is mourning a pet is this: "Suck it up and get a new one. It will relieve the grief and the pain to focus that energy into the spirit of a new animal."

Jake learned this the hard way with his beloved rescue dog Bess. When Bess was only a few years old, her aggressive behavior increasingly made her a danger to other animals and to humans. Jake adored her, and she was loving toward him, but she attacked a carpenter, mauled a neighbor's puppy, and she would escape the yard and chase people to the point that they had to jump on top of cars to get away from her. Jake could have put her up for adoption, but he says he couldn't take the responsibility of knowing that Bess would likely attack another person, pet, or an infant.

"She was like my child," Jake says. "I couldn't bear the notion of taking her to the vet and having her put down in a cold room with a stranger."

Being a doctor, Jake knew the "basics" of how to put a dog down comfortably, so he drove Bess into the mountains to go on a hike they often took together, so she would be in a place she knew and loved. "It was very psychologically trying," Jake says. "I was bawling toward the end of the hike."

He sat by a riverbed with her, and when she passed away quietly, Jake buried her by that river. He took a large stone that was the same color as Bess's fur, and years later, he still has that "football sized" stone outside in his garden.

"I don't even think my wife knows where that stone came from," he says.

For Jake, this was a more loving option than dropping his dog off with a stranger. You can have vets come to your home, which he says can be a pricey option that's not feasible for many people.

"I don't even pretend to think that a normal person would be able to do that," Jake says of putting Bess down. "It is intense. Everyone is different, but I consider our dogs family. I lost both parents, my dad when I was young and my mom two years ago, and I equate losing a pet with losing a sibling. I consider that family bond so deep and trusting, it leaves this huge gaping hole in your life. The house feels empty, like a family member is gone. In my experience it's clear that animals have a complex consciousness, so the loss may as well be the same."

Maybe Jake should travel back in time, and have a few words with Monsieur Descartes, who may have been reincarnated into the world's most cherished, intelligent, and empathetic canine. As Sakakeeny says, what you yearn to believe is what you believe. In that case, I firmly believe that René Descartes, legendary French philosopher and inventor of analytic geometry, is stuck in a never-ending loop of being reincarnated into different pets, until he comes to his senses, wises up, and finally realizes, like modern philosophers Dolly Parton and Chris Stapleton, that, beyond a shadow of a doubt, a dog has a soul.

Chapter 9
A Piece in the Puzzle

There's an old graveyard in Georgetown, Texas, just north of Austin, and toward the center sits a dual headstone. On one side the engraving reads *Sydney Augustus 1857–1858*, and on the other, *Infant Son Feb 12 1869*. Every tombstone tells a story, and as I wandered through that historic cemetery one December day in 2021, this one caught my eye. According to the inscription, these boys were the *sons of C.A.D. and A.C. Clamp.* Staring at that weathered headstone, I imagined the mother's heartache, during a time when parents likely were expected to get on with it, and not burden others with the depths of their grief. What was A.C. Clamp's day-to-day life like? How did she cope? Was C.A.D. supportive? Did she have anyone to talk to back then, about her losses? I lingered there, sending a silent acknowledgment to A.C. in hopes that maybe, somehow, it might reach her. Bonds between parents transcend centuries, lifestyles, and logic, and I felt the need to give that mom a little shout.

Most parents don't have to witness a 164-year-old tombstone to imagine the agony of losing a child. We live with that phantom fear every day. The second you are responsible for a child, and usually even before the baby is in your arms, that fear becomes part of your life. It's on your mind each time you annoy your kids by yelling, "Wear your helmet!" or "Step away from the poison berries!" Every body of water, each busy street, signals potential disaster. We have to learn to live with that anxiety in order to function, and not to turn our kids into terrified balls of neuroses, clinging to our legs every time they encounter a seesaw or a stranger. We manage the worry, and attempt to coexist with the low hum of dread it weaves throughout our lives.

"It's your worst nightmare."

My dad told me this when I finally got the courage to ask him a direct question about losing my sister. We talk about Jackie all the time, but this was different. I wanted to know how he managed to wake up each day, and find moments of joy, after experiencing this nightmare we all fear, and that we're so afraid to speak about. The day we went to visit Jackie at the funeral home, I remember him saying, "I don't think I'm ever going to be the same after this." The admission scared me. He was our sturdy oak, even after losing our mom. If he wasn't the same, what did that mean for us, and for any sense of stability we had left? We could not take one more loss, and losing our dad—if not physically, then emotionally—was unfathomable.

"It's just something where every time I try to get happy, it comes into my mind," he told me. "Will I ever be the same?

No, never. It's something you just have to live with, even when you're wondering how your heart can go on."

It's not easy to hear this from my own father. When he aches, I ache. His honesty helps me understand what he's going through, though, and I would rather him be up front with me so we can do this together, rather than pretending that things are just fine. It's that kind of honesty that helps other parents feel connected, and not ignored or pushed aside. My dad doesn't trudge through life joylessly. He works, he plays golf and goes to the gym and shows up to all of his grandkids' baseball games. He dates. We have plenty of laughs and late nights drinking red wine while listening to him play "House of the Rising Sun" on his old acoustic guitar. About a year after Jackie died, though, my sisters and I could sense the sadness in him growing deeper. During the previous months, we would tell people how strong he was, how well he was handling everything. Then we learned he was only sleeping about four hours a night, at best. He became quieter than usual. He slouched under the weight of his grief, even as he attempted to have a good time. He said that with my mom, the grief hit him immediately, but with Jackie, after the initial devastation, he "went on autopilot." He had responsibilities, like work and grandkids and kids, to think about. But you can't go on autopilot from grief for long.

"Life has enough ups and downs without losing a child," my dad says. "When you're having to carry that with you the rest of your life, it's like, How do you get through it? It's an empty feeling, and you get angry. You try to stay as healthy as you can, and I've had grief therapy. Thank god for that."

The therapy, whether it's a grief group or with individual counseling, has been a lifeline for him. He works for himself, so he can take a day off to zone out and watch *Yellowstone* or go on a long walk if he needs to. He also has three daughters constantly checking in on him, and grandkids with plenty of games and recitals to keep him engaged, so his support systems are robust. In that sense, he's fortunate. Those support systems, and the flexibility of his work, are critical for his well-being. Not everyone has those options. For some, taking time off work to grieve for a child might mean they lose their job.

Evermore, the nonprofit run by Joyal Mulheron that aims to transform bereavement policies and research in America, estimates that about 18.7 million Americans have experienced the death of a child. When Mulheron was pregnant with her third child, she was told that her baby had a chromosomal abnormality that would affect the baby's digestive system. Mulheron understood that if her child, Eleanora, made it through the pregnancy and delivery, she would likely be seriously ill, and her life would last not years, but weeks or months. Mulheron and her family decided to bring Eleanora home when she was born, which meant caring for her daughter around the clock, and experiencing terrifying moments when she thought her baby was dying, but which, for a time, turned out to be false alarms. Most days, Mulheron couldn't remember if she had showered, or if she'd eaten or taken a sip of water.

Eleanora died just before she turned five months old. During the months she was caring for her daughter, Mulheron was asked to resign from her position at work. The experience eventually inspired her to create Evermore, and to try to help anyone suffering from grief by changing the systems that so often treat the bereaved like yet another product on the assembly line. Like many parents, taking some sort of action helps them live with devastating loss. It gives them a purpose, and keeps them connected to their child. Mulheron wants to make sure that everyone, including parents who have lost children, are supported and cared for during the most difficult moments of their lives.

"People deserve honesty," Mulheron told me when I asked what the early days and months were like after Eleanora died. "It's *really* hard. The slog is hard and it is long. Whomever you lose, it becomes part of your life. It's an evolution, as far as how that person becomes woven into the fabric of you. It's not like you're going to wake up and have closure. There's no closure. You're not going to 'heal.' You didn't skin your knee."

I know I'm projecting over one hundred years into the past, but I'm sure that A.C. Clamp didn't experience "closure." She probably had to get right back to churning butter and salting deer meat, but those baby boys were likely in her heart and on her mind until the day she died. She went on living nearly fifty years after she lost her sons, which goes back to that central question: How does a parent go on after losing a child? How is it possible, not to find closure or to "heal," but to function as a human in the world? It's a question I was scared to ask my father, or any parent. It's too much, too daunting, too scary. This is the problem, though. Many parents say they've felt cast aside or alienated from friends or family who avoided speaking to them about their loss. They felt like pariahs, walking reminders of a "parent's worst nightmare." Their presence, at times, caused others to turn away.

Elizabeth Brady, a professor at Penn State whose son Mack died of a rare blood disorder just before his ninth birthday, says she eventually had to help people understand that saying nothing was the absolute worst thing they could do. Asking her how she was doing was not an assault. It was a way for her to feel seen in her pain.

"Now that I'm wearing this longer, I'm more confident about recognizing the fear and discomfort of other people," she says. "I say to my friends, 'Don't be afraid to show up, but you're not there to fix anything.' I tell them that they're there to share in the pain, and that this is just the beginning of a new life for all of us. It's a long haul. It's the rest of our lives. There is no magic card or word or anything that will fix the situation."

Over time, Brady and her husband found that talking about Mack and keeping him present in their lives helped them process their grief.

"Could you imagine not speaking about your partner, your work, your family?" she says. "We talk about the things we love."

It took Brady a while before she knew how to answer one of the most common questions any parent gets: *How many kids do you have?* She tells people she has two children, her daughter and her son Mack, who died.

"I don't hesitate anymore," Brady says. "He's still part of our family."

I've felt that hesitation many times since my sister died, when people ask if I have siblings. I stumble over my words while I figure out if I should tell them I have three sisters but one died, or do I just say I have three sisters, and leave it at that? Or do I say two? What's my emotional state at that moment, and what's theirs? How much do I want to go into this right now? Those thoughts spiral through my mind whenever the question comes up. It used to be so simple. Growing up, we were "the Gachman girls." Four, not three. It was always a thing, that my parents had four daughters, no sons. *How crazy! Your poor father! FOUR?!* We were a gaggle of girls, and without Jackie, I've struggled with what to say. Hearing Brady talk about Mack helps me realize that I can, and should, say, "I have three sisters," because I do, and always will. Whether I feel like talking about Jackie at that moment is up to me.

When a loss isn't universally acknowledged or validated by society, it can lead to disenfranchised grief. This can often be the case with miscarriage, stillbirth, or abortion, which causes many people to feel the need to stay quiet about their pain for fear of being dismissed. For Ali Smith, finding a safe space to openly speak about her grief took some time.

"I remember the trauma being all-consuming," says Smith, a New York–based photographer. She experienced four miscarriages when she was trying to have a second child, and she had no idea how to process the grief she felt. "It was such a bizarre, sad, gutting private hell. I didn't understand how to cross that bridge," Smith says of finding ways to understand or even talk about her pain. Her husband regularly went to the New York Zen Center, and Smith heard about a Buddhist ceremony there called *mizuko kuyo*, the same ceremony that Jan Chozen Bays leads at the Great Vow Zen monastery in Oregon. The ritual was originally intended for miscarriage, stillbirth, and abortion, and in many places, it has been expanded to include all children (and, of course, beloved pets). Smith says that participating in that ceremony gave her a path forward. It made her feel seen and understood, instead of feeling alone, in her private hell.

Hearing the stories of others helped her as well. "It was good to feel for someone else in those moments," she says.

Empathy is healing, and she was able to connect with strangers in that crowded room in a way that she hadn't been able to in her everyday life. One part of the ceremony is writing the name of the child on a piece of paper, and listening as the abbot, or whomever is leading the ritual, reads each and every name aloud. For the first time, Smith was able to name all four of the children she lost.

"I wouldn't say it was mystical, but those names were in me somewhere," she says. "It made me feel so much less alone that they acknowledged this reality for me. Even talking to my friends, I might feel melodramatic telling them the names of these children, so what I took from it was that my losses were real; they weren't some vaporous thing. They were valid. I can't say it cured my grief, but it was a piece in the puzzle."

Dr. Damita Sunwolf LaRue, the Chicago-based grief counselor, says she and her colleagues work with many parents who have experienced the loss of a child, and that "The reality is that it's such an intense process. It's hard to feel like you're understood." It's the loss of the "physical being" but also of the expectations you had for this child, of the things you wanted to give them or share with them, your hopes of watching them grow and evolve. She also sees several clients experiencing grief caused by fertility issues. LaRue tells people that it's important to find a community that understands their specific loss, to help them navigate their emotions and experiences.

"The world at large tends to say, 'Are you done yet?'" LaRue says of society's penchant to rush people into some sort of mythical closure. She says that this push to "get over" grief causes some parents to "edit themselves," and not speak of their loss, even though they desperately want and need connection. "Don't edit yourself. Be yourself," LaRue tells parents. "If you're at Thanksgiving and all of a sudden you're feeling sad, you should be able to say that and not worry about the reactions. That's hard because we're not raised or trained to be super real and own it when it comes up. People are holding onto so much, though, and they need to share."

Tell that to Plutarch. The ancient Greek philosopher, born in 46 CE, wrote a letter of consolation to his wife, Timoxena, after the death of their two-year-old daughter. He writes, "It is an impious thing to lament for those whose souls pass immediately into a better and more divine state." He's basically telling his wife how to mourn, and advising her not to share or get too emotional about it. My first thought when I read his letter to Timoxena was, "Screw Plutarch." How could he tell his own wife to suck it up, when they had just lost a child? He had the nerve to write to the mother of his children that their two-year-old daughter was in a "better" place. What kind of heartless, mansplaining monster was this titan of history?

Then again, this was ancient Greece, so maybe I needed to check myself and not judge the man from my vantage point centuries in the future. There must have been some anthropological explanation for his smug tone. I reached out to Lauri Reitzammer, an associate professor in the Classics Department at the University of Colorado at Boulder, for some context. I was confident that she would be able to defend his words, based on cultural norms of the time, or else she would enlighten me about some empathetic subtext that I just wasn't seeing.

"He totally comes off as an asshole," Reitzammer said when I explained my gut reaction to Plutarch's letter. I told her that it sounded to me like he was basically telling his wife, *Hey, little lady, don't embarrass us in public.*

"That's exactly what he's saying," Reitzammer said. Plutarch had just been named a priest at the Temple of Apollo in Delphi, so the guy was worried about his image, and this was not a private note about his own grief. It was a public document. The ancient version of a self-serving Twitter thread. Public lamentations of grief were common in ancient Greece, especially among women, but Reitzammer says that many men at the time were anxious about women lamenting so openly and honestly, as if it were a "dangerous force." Greek tragedy is overflowing with loss and dramatic expressions of loss, but apparently, Plutarch was not having any of it. Any modern-day grief counselor would tell him to stop trying to control Timoxena, and to get into therapy himself ASAP.

Thankfully, my dad is nothing like Plutarch. He speaks to other parents about coping with a child who has substance abuse issues and about his own experience with loss. At Bo's Place, where he sought grief counseling, he also created a small memorial plot, dedicated to my mom and my sister.

Mulheron created Evermore. Elizabeth Brady and her husband Christian started an annual soccer clinic in Mack's name, in honor of the sport he loved. It helps them feel close to Mack and keep his memory alive for generations of kids who may not have even been born when their son was here.

If establishing an annual event or launching an organization aimed at revolutionizing bereavement policy in America feels daunting, you could do something else, something simple, like buy a star.

LaRue has lost two children, and to honor them, she decided to buy an actual star gleaming up there in the night sky, and name it after all four of her children, in their birth order: Alexis, Andrew, Jerimiah, Rachael. She has a picture of this star in her house, with coordinates showing exactly where it's located in the galaxy. Seeing the star each morning is healing for her. "It's also affordable," she says. You can register a star for about $50, which is a pretty good deal when it comes to buying real estate in the cosmos.

"Waking up to that picture every morning makes me feel wonderful in my heart," LaRue says. "It's important to find a ritual that's unique to your beliefs, and this is where my Cherokee stuff comes out. I'm all about ritual."

LaRue once visited the planetarium in Chicago and asked them to show her the star named after her children. After all, she had the exact coordinates in the galaxy, so how hard could it be? When they questioned her, she had to convince them to find it.

"They were being logical and I was like, you don't understand emotion. Just show me the star and shut up."

I often think about LaRue's star, and about Brady saying that she "doesn't hesitate anymore" when people ask her how many children she has. Brady's words make answering the question "How many siblings do you have?" just a little bit easier for me. It's still tough, but I can recognize how much courage it takes for her to face those questions head-on, and not stay silent in an attempt to make someone else more comfortable. As LaRue says, everyone should be able to speak about their deepest losses. We need to be able to tell our stories, admit our fears, and ask the planetarium manager to show us the damn star. Parents, especially the ones feeling disenfranchised or alone, need to feel that they can talk about their losses without judgment, without the fear of being shut out or dismissed.

"The process of going from complete devastation to being able to have an optimistic outlook on life does not happen overnight, and sometimes it doesn't happen for a few years," says Joyal Mulheron. "It can be a slow evolution. What I would say to other parents is be patient with yourself and give yourself the same permission you would have granted your loved one to feel what you're feeling and cope with what you're feeling. Be relentlessly patient with yourself."

I'll never know if A.C. Clamp was patient with herself, or what the pieces in the puzzle were for her to go on living with her losses. I do know that she's more than just a name on an old tombstone. Her story matters. She was a parent, a person. Someone whose grief, like that of so many millions of others, is forever valid, as real as the etchings on that stone.

Chapter 10
'Til Death Do Us Part
(Please Wear Sunscreen
and Get a Colonoscopy)

The night my husband proposed to me, I told him I planned to live to be 100 years old. It was an arbitrary number, but it meant that he had to hang on until he was 102 so we could die together in bed, like (Spoiler Alert!) the couple in *The Notebook*, the Nicholas Sparks book–turned–movie that ends with the lovers cuddling in bed and dying peacefully in their sleep, spooning for all eternity. I was trying to be flirty and cute when I made this declaration, but I also think there was an element of fear there. When you pledge to spend your life with someone, whether that involves marriage and legal documents or a promise and a kiss, the hope is that you will grow old together. Despite our best intentions and loftiest goals, there is one outcome that is 100 percent guaranteed in romance and in life. Each one of us will, at some point, take our last breath. Chances are high that this final bow will not happen while you're dancing a tango with your true love under a moonlit sky in Argentina, only to be struck by a single bolt of lightning, which takes you both down gracefully, intertwined forevermore. It does sound romantic, though. Ridiculous and beyond the realm of all possibility, but romantic.

As I've gotten older, instead of fantasizing about rapturous love affairs and Hollywood endings, I'm begging my husband to get a colonoscopy and wear sunscreen.

Before I met Jerett, I spent years dating in Los Angeles and had started to accept—and even embrace—the fact that I might just go through life on my own, which meant having a career, supporting myself, and maybe adopting a child one day. I was certain that my chances of meeting someone in that city who actually wanted a committed relationship were about as promising as my chances of waking up as Daphne Brigerton, when she was still the most eligible bachelorette in Regency London. So when I met Jerett and he turned out to be a handsome Jewish triathlete doctor who was funny, kind, and not allergic to commitment, it was a surprise. We were no strangers to dating and, in turn, to relationships toppling with the speed of a domino line, so we were both pretty jaded when our paths magically crossed (thanks to online dating). But there we were, falling in love. In the middle of Los Angeles, a city of eight million humans, I had found the one person I would (hopefully) drop dead with after all.

My parents never experienced the complexities of dating in a huge, sprawling city where getting ghosted is—I'm guessing here—99 percent more common than getting a proposal. My mother and father met in high school and fell

Things That Might Seem Like Nagging, But That Actually Mean "I Love You—Please Don't Die"

- Be careful using that table saw. You could chop your hand off.

- If you don't sell your motorcycle, I'm leaving you.

- You're swimming too far out, come back!

- Please make an appointment to get that checked.

- Why are you driving so fast?

- Why didn't you call me? I was worried.

- Put on your helmet/life vest/seat belt/knee pads.

- Take these vitamins.

- Do you really think you should be skydiving/ spelunking/BASE jumping at your age?

- And my favorite: I need you to stay around a long time. Until you're 102.

in love as teenagers, so they didn't really date, at least not in the way we think of dating today. As teenagers, my parents had fun, but they also got into legendary arguments that caused my mom to rip my dad's black and white, 8x10 senior picture in half and then tape it back together again, multiple times. When I asked my dad what drove him to wed so young, he said, "Your mom wanted to get married and have a family, and I didn't want to lose her." So he proposed.

When my parents married at just nineteen, back in 1970, they had no crystal ball showing them that my mom would be diagnosed with a terminal illness at sixty-five years old. If that sounds old to you, it definitely is not. Wait until you're fifty or sixty, and you'll see. As of the writing of this book, Halle Berry is fifty-five, and no one in their right mind would categorize her as *old*. The point is, my parents experienced decades of love, growth, and change, and they deserved so many more. They expected to grow old together and watch their grandchildren go from infants to kids to teens, and beyond. They hoped for that outcome, but as Joan Didion writes of her husband John Gregory Dunne's sudden death from a heart attack in *The Year of Magical Thinking*, "Life changes fast. Life changes in the instant. You sit down to dinner and life as you know it ends."

For my parents, that instant happened the moment my mom was diagnosed with stage IV colon cancer.

"We were so young when we got married, and you think you're immortal at twenty or twenty-one," my dad says. "I figured we would grow old together, until she was diagnosed. Even then, I still hoped."

My dad was by her side every single day for those difficult years, devoted, committed, altering his diet to match hers so she wouldn't get depressed eating ketogenic foods or the BRAT diet (bananas, rice, applesauce, toast) while he gorged on a Porterhouse and some Chianti. They still argued, like the time she was pissed that he didn't want to spring for a more expensive wig for her. She enlisted her daughters to launch a verbal assault, and we each explained to him why a nice wig was extremely important. The nice wig looked like her own hair. It didn't seem fake, or make her feel insecure. Kathryn, who went with our mom to try on the cheaper wig, told our dad that she looked like Dudley Moore when she put it on. We're skilled when it comes to applying just the right amount of pressure, so he ended up coming around, eventually. No offense to the late, great Dudley Moore, whose shag hairdo suited him perfectly.

During those years, my father spent his days making doctors' appointments, searching every corner of the internet for experimental procedures, reminding my mom to take her medications, and holding her hand when she was scared, which was often. He researched and bought so many vitamins and supplements for her that when we would call to see how she was doing, she'd say, "If your father says *keto* or *turmeric* one more time, I'm going to hit him over the head with a frying pan."

No matter how much she hated it, though, she tried anything she could, whatever vitamins my father brought home, until there was nothing anyone, or anything, could do.

They were in it together, until the last instant. The morning she died, when we were gathered around her at home, was the first time I had ever heard my dad call my mom "baby." I knew they loved each other, but that simple word telegraphed something deeper, something private. Hearing him say it crushed me. We were losing our mom, and he was losing the woman he'd loved since he was a teenager, the most beautiful person in the world to him, the funniest, the wisest, the most infuriating, the one he cherished. He was losing part of himself.

As I grew up and wised up, my parents replaced the storybook romances as a couple to admire. They weren't perfect. My dad never scaled a balcony before a date like Shakespeare's Romeo. His M.O. was to saunter up to the front door shockingly late. He loved adventure, and my mom loved a nice hotel room. He watched old John Wayne Westerns like *The Searchers*, and she was devoted to classic Hollywood. My mom, being a decorator, loved beautiful things. My dad would have been happy in a room with a brown leather chair, a television, and a duct-taped remote. She secretly threw out his worn, tattered, brown reclining chair one day, and he was so furious when he found out you would have thought she told him she'd been having a twenty-year affair with the neighbor. They argued during the early years of my sister being in and out of rehabs, and the stresses of that time took a toll on their marriage. Despite any challenges, though, their love endured.

It was because they were imperfect that I started to understand what marriage could be. It wasn't flowers and fainting spells. It was the day-to-day choice to walk through life together, no matter what hardships might reveal themselves down the road. Flowers were a bonus, but flowers wilt.

A few weeks before I got married, I texted my mom to see if she had any last-minute advice. I wanted to know if she cried at her wedding. I hoped for a sweet story about her tearstained veil. Maybe she gazed into my father's eyes and felt a powerful burst of emotional fireworks, mixed with a cocoon-like safety, assuring her that he was The One. When I asked her if she cried, she texted:

no.
We were too young and dumb!

My parents didn't have end-of-life caregiving or hospice arrangements on their mind when they got married. My dad still had his green and chrome 1971 Triumph 500 motorcycle, which my mom would eventually guilt him into selling, out of that same desire that I have to keep my husband around as long as possible. It's not healthy to spend your relationship worrying about the other person dying, but as you get older, those worries tend to creep in. My parents spent so much of their youth together. They had fun, they argued, they worked it out. They were best friends. If any couple seemed like they were on the path to one day literally cuddling to death as in *The Notebook*, it was them.

When I asked my dad if he felt "young and dumb" on their wedding day, like my mom, he said, "Yeah. I'm about to turn twenty years old and I'm getting married? Holy crap. I was a little nervous."

Oh, to be young and dumb forever. But, as Shakespeare's Juliet would say, *Alas!* The Census Bureau's 2020 American Community Survey estimates that over 1 million women and 458,905 men became widowed during the preceding five years. The word *census* aside, those are not just numbers. They're people of all ages who have lost soul mates, best friends, co-parents, and companions. How each of those people handles their grief is different. Maybe some wait a few years and then tiptoe into dating again. Others might choose to never partner up, since they had their person and they don't feel that falling in love again would add anything to their lives. A few might remarry soon after their loss. In any of these cases, you can pretty much guarantee that there will be relationship advice given and judgment passed by family, friends, neighbors, and your hairdresser.

My paternal grandfather was devastated when my grandmother died from complications of Parkinson's, but he remarried about a year later. I was just out of high school, and I remember feeling angry at first, probably because I wanted to be loyal to my grandmother. That changed the first time I saw him giggle with his wife, Carole. I was happy that he had someone to love and to share his life with. It helped that she was one of those people who are just so damn kind, and not in a cloying, phony way. She was bubbly, joyful, and hilarious, often without meaning to be. If they handed out Nobel Peace Prizes for possessing a sweet, pure soul, she would absolutely have been flown to Sweden to accept her award. Seeing my grandfather and Carole happy for so many years after my grandmother died made me believe that maybe it was pretty simple, this whole concept of "moving on" after loss. There was hope for us all. This assumption was problematic, though. It took me several years to understand the many reasons why.

I've watched my own father, alone after forty-eight years of marriage, struggling to "get back out there." It did not help that when he stepped into the dating world, two years after my mom passed away, he, a seventy-year-old grandfather, naively created a profile on Tinder. As in, "twenty-three-year-olds trying to hook up at midnight on a Tuesday" Tinder. In his defense, he said it was the only app he'd heard about, so he figured that's what everyone used. The guy hadn't been on a date since Richard Nixon was president and the Delfonics were on the *Billboard* charts, so I believed him.

When my sisters and I found out about his choice of dating platform, we immediately employed scorched-earth tactics to stop him, by any means necessary. The man we had placed on a pedestal for decades, the one who accompanied us to daddy-daughter dances and walked us down the aisle at our weddings, could not, under any circumstances, swipe right on anyone who was not an age-appropriate, kind, genuine, self-sufficient, funny, empathetic, confident, fun-loving human being. Was that so much to ask? That this unknown person be close to perfect?

Once we won the battle of the dating apps, we walked by our father's side as he explored other avenues and apps. As hard as it was to imagine him dating other women, let alone marrying another woman, the last thing we wanted was for him to feel lonely. My sisters and I had our kids and our spouses to keep us busy, and he had an empty house that he once shared with our mother. He was surrounded by photos and memories. He did have his elderly Hemingway cat, but she was perpetually grouchy and a terrible conversationalist.

Now, my sisters and I can laugh off the early struggles we had with our dad starting to date, but in reality it was a tough journey for all of us. Adjusting to a world we didn't ask for, one where my father might possibly go out with women, meant we had to put his needs before whatever anxieties or sorrow or anger we felt. It meant we had to support him—within limits, of course. If he showed me a dating profile photo of a stunning woman posing in Lululemon workout gear who said she was sixty-five but looked thirty, I laid down the law. Once, he sent me a photo of a woman who said she was in her sixties, and he asked me what I thought. It was an

Instagram photo someone had stolen from one of the *Selling Sunset* stars, who was in her early thirties, at most. Another "woman" kept texting him things that sounded like they were coming straight from the mouth of a sexy Russian bot:

> I mowing lawn today. How is your lovely day today?
> Send more photos will you please sir?

The only thing these bots don't ask for is his social security number. This type of exchange is not a rarity, by the way. I have become a veritable expert at detecting online dating scams from a mile away. It's my new superpower.

Above all else, I want my dad to live a long, healthy life, and, as a society, we are constantly told that loneliness is not at the top of the longevity must-have lists. My grandfather lived until ninety-five (and traveled and played golf until he was ninety-four), possibly because he found love again and he had a companion to go to movies and dinner with. It's also possible that he was just blessed with good health. I've heard that older people who lose spouses are at much higher risk of dying themselves, what's known as the "widowhood effect." A 2006 study, published in the *New England Journal of Medicine*, found that 49 percent of husbands and 30 percent of wives died in the nine years following the death of their spouse. Another study, published in 2013 in the *Journal of Public Health*, involved 12,316 participants, who were married from 1998 through 2008. Researchers found that in the first three months after losing a spouse, their risk of premature death increased by 66 percent.

If you're a romantic and you believe in love, it's hard not to also believe that losing your partner would potentially carry you out, too. All these studies and articles about the "widowhood effect" do not help, since they instill in us a mortal fear of losing our partner, giving us anxiety and making us believe that if they go, our demise might be just around the corner.

My dad is, thankfully, healthy and active, so the goal is to keep him happy, thriving, and alive for as long as possible, not to sabotage his chances of finding love again. And so, for the past few years, we've tried our best to help him sift through catfish scams and lawn-mowing bots to find something, not perfect, but real. It's not always easy. I was once asked during a live radio interview how I would feel if my dad dated someone my own age. In an effort to mask my horror, my face contorted into a smile so pained and plastered, I'm pretty sure I looked like the Joker from *Batman*. It was radio, so no one could see me, but my discomfort was so intense people could no doubt hear it radiating through the speakers.

"Your dad could easily end up on a date with somebody like seven or eight years older than you. Will that freak you out? Will you yell at him? What will happen if that happens?" the interviewer asked.

His barrage of questions was followed by my Joker grin, an awkward pause, a deep sigh, and several seconds of me stumbling all over my words before I managed to utter, "I don't think I'd handle that so well." Then I basically blacked out until the next question came my way.

"We're all five years old in our brain when it comes to family," says Chicago-based psychologist LaRue. In her practice, she's observed that "almost everyone has gotten pushback from adult children or kids or friends" when it comes to dating again after losing a partner. My sisters and I support our dad, but that doesn't mean we don't revert to our five-year-old selves if we think a woman we've never met doesn't seem right for him, simply because she ordered a wedge salad instead of a real meal. We've scolded him for not texting a woman back soon enough, for texting too soon, and for taking someone to a fancy dinner on the first date. ("Just have coffee or a drink, in case you don't get along! You have to think of your retirement savings!") One of my sisters who shall remain nameless has repeatedly Google- and Facebook-stalked women my dad has gone out with, and her sleuthing skills are no joke ("Her son went to high school with my friend Luke's brother, and he said she's evil. She's a cheap tipper . . ."). We critique these women's clothes ("Why is this woman wearing a hot pink tube top? She's sixty not sixteen . . ."). We judge them on a profile photo ("Dad, this woman is sitting on Hugh Hefner's lap . . .").

My dad's response to that last observation?

"Well, maybe they were good friends? Or maybe they're related."

In addition to scrutinizing these women's outfits, meals, and life choices, we also always compare them to our mom, which isn't at all fair, but neither is the fact that she's gone, and we have been forced to serve as our father's virtual, judgmental, highly picky wing women. We were more relentless in the beginning, but we've since calmed down. For the most part.

Once we laid down our arms about his choice of apps, I got used to asking my dad about his latest date. We were thankful that he was engaged in the world, instead of retreating and becoming a statistic. Along the way, I have explained what ghosting is, and listened as he's grappled with conflicting emotions, like having a great time with someone, but still missing our mom when he comes back home. We've scrolled through dating apps together, and I've helped him pick photos and write his profile, since, left to his own devices, he put his name, age, religion, and nothing else, like a devout, reticent stalker.

He also tried an in-person dating service that set him up on blind dates. Some of those experiences were fine; most could be classified as "interesting."

He went on one blind date with a woman who, in the middle of dinner, said, "I've been dating a while but I'm picky because I'm pretty pleasing to the eye, as you know."

"Well, yes, you are . . ." my dad said, not knowing how else to respond. She was pretty, but evidently also pretty cocky. At that point, he knew this was a single glass of wine situation.

"When we walked out of the restaurant, she did this little twirl, turning around in a complete circle like she was telling me *See how attractive I am*," my dad told me. After that awkward moment, he said goodbye and headed home, wondering what had just happened.

"That was a one-and-done date," he said.

He did meet one widow through the dating service who was beautiful, funny, and smart. He was so excited to take her out again, but she basically ghosted him, and later told him she'd been in a long-term relationship and they were on a break when she went out with my dad, but they'd gotten back together. It was the first time he'd felt even remotely excited and hopeful about someone. I felt for him when it fizzled so quickly, but that's how dating goes. Timing is not everything, but it's a 95 percent thing.

About two years into his scrolling, my dad told me that dating was harder now than it was at the beginning. When he first started going out with women, about two years after my mom died, we were all just starting to feel that we could step back into the flow of life. For him, that meant dating. Even after Jackie died, he eventually got back out there, but then something shifted. Instead of going out and having dinner and a few laughs, he was faced with conversations about commitment, or questions about whether or not he kept my mother's photos up around the house. He met some women he had great times with, women who seemed to care about him. Still, he struggled. He would come home, even after a great date, and suddenly become weighed down by thoughts about what a sharp turn his life had taken. He wasn't sure how to navigate this new phase. When my mom was sick, they never spoke about him dating or finding love, and that also plagued him with guilt. Because of that, I make sure to tell my husband firmly and honestly, "If I die, I want you to be happy. I want you to meet someone else. Hopefully, it's your 'hall pass' Marisa Tomei." I'm not sure why I feel the need to repeat this as often as I do. I'm sure once is enough, but I do not want to wind up dead and full of guilt, hovering overhead while watching my widower husband mope around all day because he feels that he can't get coffee with another woman.

"It's strange," my dad says. "Forty-eight years is a lot of years to be married. What gets me is being home at night. I'm alone and talking to myself, but that's not a reason to just go jump into a serious thing with a lady I'm not enamored with."

He started to realize that he wasn't ready for a relationship, not because he was a wannabe twenty-three-year-old lothario, but because his grief was still too raw, too present. He was processing not just the loss of his wife, but the loss of one of his children. It's hard to let a new person into that experience, especially if they haven't dealt with such deep loss in their own life.

"Before, I could go out on dates even though I still had grief," he told me. "I felt like I needed a life, and I didn't want to sit in the house every night. My grief counselor told me it was healthy to have a social life." After my sister died, though, he noticed that his sleep patterns were getting worse. He felt increasingly anxious throughout the day. His thoughts raced at night.

So he decided that he needed to take a break from dating to process his grief and get his sleep habits under control.

"What they say about grief is that it hits you the most when you're starting to feel the best," he says. "For a while, you have all this adrenaline, and then it's like your brain says it's payback time."

Once my dad took this break to reconsider whether he even wanted to marry again, I started to check my own biases. I assumed, like our culture hammers into us with terms like the "widowhood effect," that in order for my dad to live a happy, fulfilled life he needed to find love again. Loneliness isn't the answer, but assuming that you're destined to endure a life that's lacking just because you don't marry the first person you go on a date with isn't the answer, either. Not everyone needs or wants to remarry—or marry in the first place. Marriage rates are on the decline, so it's not as if you're doomed to a short, unhappy life if you never date or remarry after loss. Despite what the studies say, there are plenty of perpetually single people who live long, fabulous lives. Joan Didion lived for eighteen years after her husband died, until she was eighty-seven, and she never remarried. If my dad wants a relationship, I'll support him. If he doesn't, I'll support him in that, too.

When I asked my dad if he thought he would date again after his hiatus, he told me, "I'm charting a new path for myself, which I never thought I'd have to do."

My dad keeps going to grief counseling, and, as of now, he'll consider dating again when he feels he's mentally and emotionally ready.

My brother-in-law Niall, Jackie's husband, told me that a year after she died, he realized he would come home to the Colorado apartment they shared and just "walk in circles." He didn't mean it as a metaphor. He was trapped in that place, full of memories, caught in a cycle of trying to process what happened. Despite their struggles, Niall and Jackie deeply loved each other. They first met at a restaurant in New York "around 10 a.m. on a Tuesday," he says. He spotted Jackie, and asked their mutual friend Mike to introduce them. It was love at first sight.

"We hit it off," Niall says. "Mike, who is a big talker, couldn't get another word in. I really did find her beautiful and funny. We talked about everything. It was such a great day for both of us."

They went to AA meetings together, cooked dinner, and shared a love of animals. When they moved in together, into a tiny railroad-style apartment in Queens, they had one little white fluffy dog named Tony, and one giant Burmese Mountain dog named Sally that took up half the living room. When Jackie and Niall were sober together, they had a good life, meeting friends for dinner or watching movies at home. When they weren't sober, things quickly turned tumultuous, but they always found their way back to each other. In a photo of their wedding at City Hall, their bodies are facing forward but they're gazing over at each other, and the adoration in their eyes is clear. I love that photo, because my sister, who sometimes appeared lost or detached in pictures, looks truly happy, present, and radiant.

After over a year spent pacing in his Colorado apartment, one day in spring 2022 Niall packed his things, loaded his car, and left that small town. He told me he drove straight through to New York, barely stopping. He hoped to eventually make his way to his home country, Ireland, a place my sister always wanted to visit with him. Niall became a widower in his mid-forties, and says he doesn't know if he'll remarry. He's just trying to navigate this new phase of his life, without her.

"I'm in a better place to get the help I need," Niall told me. "Jackie was the light of my life, and I'll never forget that."

I hope he finds happiness, whatever that means for him. I hope the memory of my sister can bring him comfort one day, so that he can stop walking in circles, and find some peace.

LaRue, the Chicago-based psychologist, told me about one widow she was counseling, who had put her own mental and physical health aside for years to care for her ailing husband.

When he passed away, one of the goals they worked on was for this woman to take care of herself, which meant scheduling doctors' visits, exercising, sleeping when she needed to, and going out and being social when she could. For widows and widowers, that kind of self-care can come with a whole lot of guilt, which LaRue helps them work through.

"You're not doing anything wrong by taking care of yourself," she says. "It doesn't mean your grief will go away."

Another patient in LaRue's practice, who was dying, wrote a "manifesto" for her husband, telling him to take care of himself and their children, and urging him to find love again.

"She wrote that she was young, she got sick, and that eventually she wanted him to move on," LaRue recalls.

The husband started seeing LaRue as a patient, and she helped him navigate the experience of dating again, in ways that were both emotional and practical. Maybe she had to explain ghosting to him, as I did with my dad. Maybe she talked to him about the fact that even if he met someone new, his relationship with his wife would not disappear. She could have told him that finding someone who could honor his past relationship instead of feeling threatened by it would be a good first step.

Loss can take so much away from us. It can devastate us, rob us of sleep, drown us in loneliness while we're having dinner with a stranger. Days can turn into a maze of memory. A single night can stretch on so long that you want to scream, and claw for the sunlight. My dad and so many others live with this reality. No matter what may happen down the road, he holds his romance with my mom in his heart. He carries it into the next morning, the next date, the next sleepless night. The right person will, hopefully, understand that, if he chooses to find that person. This person will want to walk through life with him, never expecting him to let my mom go. She'll want to know about my mom, and ask questions, and maybe even say, "She sounds like an amazing human being. I wish I could have known her." At least, that's what I hope, for him and for us.

You can't date or marry away your loss, and you can't control your fate, or the fate of the one you love. All you can do is remind the person you love to wear sunscreen, to get a colonoscopy, and to drive a little more slowly in the rain. You can be there for each other, until the last instant. And when they're gone, you do your best. I try not to judge my dad's dating choices anymore, and I reject the notion that he'll die of loneliness if he never remarries. I just want him to do whatever his heart desires, and if his heart desires a seventy-year-old woman in a hot pink tube top? As long as she's kind, funny, self-sufficient, loyal, loving, genuine, empathetic, and patient, I think we might just get along.

Chapter 11
So Sorry for Your Loss

Over the dramatic chords of a synth imitating a church organ at the beginning of Prince's song "Let's Go Crazy," he calls out to his Dearly Beloved, like a cosmic preacher delivering the world's most rapturous eulogy. In my interpretation of those lyrics, he's telling us that we are gathered together to get through the day-to-day hardship, heartbreak, and pain of life. And we are going to damn well dance while we do it.

If anyone can inspire millions of people to dance through life's toughest moments, it's Prince. It's hard to see his signature shade of purple and not mourn his passing. In April 2016, when the world discovered that he died unexpectedly at the age of fifty-seven, the fences around Paisley Park, his estate in Minnesota, were transformed into a shrine of purple flowers, balloons, and handwritten notes. Vigils were held around the world. In Brooklyn, Spike Lee threw a block party so neighbors could come together and mourn. NASA shared a photo of a purple nebula, in his honor. The Eiffel Tower and the New Orleans Superdome were lit up in purple. In the middle of a Beyoncé show I went to in Los Angeles the month after Prince died, the stage was suddenly lit up in purple, the skyscraper-sized speakers blared "Purple Rain," and the entire audience braced for what was coming. Beyoncé reemerged in her thigh-high boots with her hair billowing in the wind machine, belting out Prince's song "The Beautiful Ones" as if she were delivering an ancient lamentation. The feeling of collective, overwhelming loss and appreciation for this person so few of us knew but all of us loved allowed us all to go crazy, in the best sense, and release our grief together, arms raised to the heavens, lighters ignited and reaching toward the sky.

In the wake of Prince's death, people traveled from all over the world to pay their respects at Paisley Park. The grief was public, visible, a shared experience felt by neighbors, friends, and strangers.

Experts call this phenomenon "collective grief," or what happens when groups of people, who may not even know each other, experience the same sense of deep sorrow, stress, and anxiety stemming from a tragedy or loss. Since we're so interconnected now, and information and images reach us all so quickly, that sense of collective grief can sometimes make it feel as if we are living through a time when the tragedies will not let up, that today is somehow worse than ever before. There's an overwhelming sense of *When will all of this end?* When can we go back to being carefree, or at least go back to feeling that there is some hope out there? Will we ever live through a twenty-four-hour news cycle that doesn't send us all into an emotional tailspin? Unless you completely unplug, there is rarely a break from all the madness.

"The year he died, I felt like I wanted to go see his home," says Ryan Beeman, a Prince fan who lived in Los Angeles at the time of Prince's death. There were several people there the day he visited Paisley Park, paying their respects, just as he was, but Beeman says the one who sticks in his mind is a woman who flew all the way to Minnesota from Italy. She stood at the gates surrounding Prince's home, in tears. She was there before he arrived, and she was still there when he left. Beeman says that of any musician who had passed away during his lifetime, Prince's death hit him the hardest: "Something about him passing tugged at my heartstrings. When he died, it kind of felt like all of us were more fragile for some reason."

With celebrities, we're allowed and even expected to be vocal in our grief. There's no shame in hosting a block party or bathing a 1,083-foot Parisian tower in royal purple light. At least in most Western societies, private grief is expected to be just that—private. Our moments of wailing in agony for the ones we love are confined to bedrooms, closets, and breakroom corners. And if you weep too loudly and too often in the breakroom corner, you might just lose your job. Crying quietly at a funeral is acceptable, but, soon after, we're expected to "go on" with life, and put the mourning rituals and outward displays of deep grief aside. Sometimes grief can and should be solitary and quiet, but, at its core, it is anything but quiet. It's a loud, relentless beast. Grief thrashes and roars, until it settles into a rhythm we can live with.

Emotions this volatile can be frightening, not just for those of us who have lived at their mercy, but for the people surrounding us—the friends and colleagues and neighbors who haven't learned this language yet, and who don't know what to say or do.

"People really shy away from grief and don't want to think or talk about it," says Dr. Katherine Shear of Columbia's Center for Prolonged Grief. "They don't want to be with people who are grieving because it's painful to be with someone who is emotionally activated. It makes them feel helpless."

Collective grief isn't a new phenomenon, obviously. Public rituals similar to the ancient Greek practice of women lamenting out in the open in response to a death still happen around the world (and at Beyoncé shows). New Orleans jazz funerals bring people together in the streets to celebrate the departed through dance, music, and movement, as a reminder that death and life are not opposites; they're part of the same cycle that binds us all. Jazz funerals, or second lines, have been held for celebrities like Prince and David Bowie, and for everyday people. Not everyone gets the Eiffel Tower lit up for them, but that doesn't mean Prince's death is more important or impactful than the death of someone's aunt, or someone's son. We've seen this through the pandemic with millions of lives lost across the world. Each one is worth lighting up the Eiffel Tower for, or celebrating in the streets, especially to the people who loved them the most.

Shear has worked with people who have lost loved ones during the pandemic, and with others who are struggling with a sense of collective grief that comes with living through a time when the world as we knew it has unraveled, and become scary, unpredictable, and unknown. They could be grieving the loss of a job, a home, a business, a way of life. A country unhinged. A brother or a best friend, a patient, a coworker, or a stranger across the world.

"A sense of shared loss is painful, but it also has the potential for comfort because you realize you're not alone," says Shear. "The more we can let grief into our national experience and everyday life as a community, the better off we will be. We need something to replace the community rituals that our ancestors may have had. You need to be able to feel that you're still connected with your social groups in a meaningful way."

Tony Pham, the meditation coach and death doula, told me that he spent a year in Vietnam after college, and he remembers seeing a funeral where the family members were openly wailing in the streets. Witnessing such a public display of grief made him realize that, in America at least, people often feel like they "need permission" to grieve.

"Ritual is a huge piece of it," he says of how he draws on other cultures and traditions to help people process their grief. "Whether you're religious or not, it's important to have some sort of reflection or process to be able to be present with what's happening."

My process when Prince died consisted of playing "Purple Rain" at full volume, watching the tributes all over the news, and scrolling Twitter and nodding in teary-eyed solidarity when someone's pithy expression of pain resonated. I also thought back to the fourth-grade musical our class wrote, directed, and starred in, with a plot that pitted Prince against Liberace in a courtroom, for some crime that is now lost on me. In my memory, it was an epic show. I was painfully shy at that time, but I inhabited my role as a singing, dancing juror as if I were an ingenue vying for a Tony Award. If anyone was capable of luring me out of my shell, it was the Purple One. We sang a medley of Prince songs at the top of our little lungs. Liberace's musical talents got short shrift, I'm afraid to say. The plot may have involved a *People's Court* situation, where these two titanic talents were suing each other over something critical, like a rhinestone-studded parking spot. Who knows. I don't remember the inspiration for this play, but God bless the teachers who drew up a lesson plan that freed us from the tyranny of multiplication tables and allowed us to dance to "Little Red Corvette"—during school, for a grade.

That was long before I knew deep loss, long before Prince's death ignited a million purple lights and brought so many of us together to mourn him, and mourn what he brought to each of our lives.

When I did finally experience true grief, right after my mother died, someone told me, "Grief is not only a complex beast, but is beautifully transcendent as well."

Similar to my initial reactions when people would say, "So sorry for your loss," my first response to these words was not, "Oh, thank you so much!" It was pure, unapologetic rage. *Transcendent?* My life was not a Ralph Waldo Emerson poem. I wasn't wandering through the woods writing odes to sunbeams, forest floors, and shy hawks. Death was not glorious and wondrous like nature; it was a blunt object, lurking in a corner. The "complex beast" part of this comment resonated with me, but the rest simmered. As the days and months went on, though, the comment stayed with me. I mulled it over in my mind, growing less angry, and more curious. No one is trying to crush your spirit when they say "So sorry for your loss" or when they tell you that grief is "transcendent." People, *in general*, mean well. So maybe there was something to this comment. Maybe this person actually understood something that I didn't.

Transcendent means "extending or lying beyond the limits of ordinary experience *or* exceeding usual limits." Those definitions didn't upset me as much as my original assumptions about sunbeams and rainbows. There is nothing pretty about grief, but, eventually, once I understood and accepted that it wasn't going to "go away," that it was not a detour, and that it would reshape my view of the world and of all the billions of humans on earth walking through these same experiences, I thought, maybe this person is right. Maybe, in addition to the soreness of the heart and the sobs so powerful you're doubled over in pain, this thing that none of us asked for, and that none of us can prevent from coming into our lives, could, possibly, open us up, strip us down, and help us connect in ways we weren't capable of before.

It can feel like this age, or the current moment in time, is defined by loss. Whether it's the death of a loved one, yet another celebrity we adore who unexpectedly died too soon, over a million Americans taken by the pandemic, another devastating mass shooting, the loss of reproductive rights, or something less tangible, like the climate crisis, it sometimes feels that we're drowning in reasons to grieve.

I didn't even realize that I was experiencing a type of climate grief, which is a psychological response to a changing environment, until I found myself taking photos of some local cows every day. I regularly passed by this field of cows on the way to pick up Cole from preschool, and each time I drove by, I felt a pang in my heart. Eventually, I realized that it was because so much of central Texas, which has historically been full of fields and open space, was quickly getting bulldozed to death to make way for homogenous housing developments and yet another gas station. I'd never had a special affinity for cows, but now the thought of this idyllic bovine scene disappearing depressed me. I took the time to print and frame a photo of those cows, and it's now hanging on the wall by my desk at home. When I glance up at the picture, I can appreciate that moment in time, a moment that appears beautiful to me largely because it feels so ephemeral.

Climate grief, or climate distress, is not a new phenomenon. Indigenous people around the world have been experiencing this particular form of loss for centuries. Now, though, 105-degree temperatures in England and random apocalyptic freezes in Texas have us all panicked. *Solastalgia*, or the distress and anxiety caused by a change in the environment, is a term coined by an Australian philosopher named Glenn Albrecht. Once I learned that term, my sudden save-the-cows anxiety made perfect sense, at least to me. Unfortunately, my solastalgia has trickled down to Cole. Like many young kids, he once loved excavators, bulldozers, backhoes, and cement mixers with a burning passion. Random construction sites were his Coachella. Now, after listening to me hem and haw every time I see a lone dump truck next to a pile of dirt, the poor kid can't even enjoy a skid steer.

"Ugh, Mommy, look! Construction. We hate construction, right?"

"Yes! We love cows and fields and flowers. No more construction!"

"Construction is *not good*. They need to stop, right?"

"Yes. But excavators are fun! Bulldozers are cool."

"Mommy! No, they're not. What about the cows?"

I haven't yet figured out whether I've done my son a favor by inadvertently teaching him about solastalgia so young, or if I've traumatized him for life. I guess time will tell. This is the eternal dilemma of parenthood. We're either setting them up for success, or ruining their lives by opening our mouths and exposing them to our own not-so-secret anxieties.

Faith Kearns, a California-based scientist and science communicator who writes about wildfires, water, and climate change, spends her days focused on dire issues that most of us attempt to distract ourselves from as we toss away our plastic cups and attempt to recycle our fifth can of peach-flavored carbonated water.

"People are always asking me how I find hope," Kearns says. "I'm generally a more pessimistic person and I don't find hope to be super interesting. But I wake up and put one foot in front of the other, and I manage my own grief."

Kearns says that if it's an unseasonably warm, sunny day in San Francisco, it's tough for her to enjoy the weather like everyone else playing Frisbee in the park because she's thinking that it *should* actually be cold and raining.

"I try to find space to enjoy what's still here, and what's beautiful, which is a lot," she says.

That's why I love my cow picture so much. I can enjoy the view, because, for now, it is still here, and still beautiful.

When things do feel overwhelming, whether that's due to the weather or a tragedy I see on the news (or both), I try to remember that it has always been this way, and for centuries people have kept going on. In the not-so-distant past, the AIDS Memorial Quilt was created to commemorate and honor the deaths caused by another pandemic that, at the time, caused a massive sense of helplessness, rage, fear, and loss around the globe. The project was conceived by gay rights activist Cleve Jones. The names of people who died of the disease were stitched together to create a giant quilt, which was first displayed in Washington, DC in 1987. There are now over 100,000 names on the quilt, and it has been shown around the globe. It's more than a symbol. It's a way for people to mourn individual and collective losses, whether you're viewing it in person or online.

Brenda Goodman, a filmmaker and professor who went to see the Memorial Quilt when it was first displayed, says she remembers "the feeling of walking along and seeing the enormity of what had happened."

Goodman went to pay her respects to friends she'd lost, and to be with other people who were mourning both personally and collectively.

"The quilt was like any time when you're dealing with ritual and dealing with something that is about remembering somebody," she says. "There are two sides of the coin. There is the sense that there's a way people can live on and be remembered, and also the feeling and awareness of the enormity of the loss that was so hard to fathom. I remember other people there that day, and there was a sense of community."

That sense of community can stem from shared feelings among thousands or millions, or among a handful of people you love.

A few years ago, some friends and I started a tradition where we get together for a three- or four-day trip, once a year. I've know these friends since we were eighteen and nineteen years old, and now we're in our forties. Our bond is as thick as a blood tie. We've been through career ups and downs, broken hearts, marriages, divorces, childbirth, fights, deaths of mutual friends and loved ones, estrangements, and forgiveness. We are linked, happily, for life.

I don't get to see them often, since I've moved to Texas and they're all in California, so I cherish any time we have together. We might talk on the phone once or twice a year, and text eight hundred times, but sharing a house and drinking wine in our pajamas allows us to take the short amount of time we have together and shed all the layers of being "just fine" that accumulate during our daily lives. Our 2020 "trip" was a luxurious tropical escape into a thirty-minute Zoom session, but now we're back, in real life, with a vengeance. We pack suitcases full of cute jumpsuits and wine. Conversations ripple and intersect. The dam breaks open and we cannot seem to stop. Calling it a "girls' trip" feels reductive, since we're grown women with careers and children and way more responsibilities than we had back when we met, but what the hell. It's a girls' trip. We take pictures of each other's face serums and squeal about charcuterie boards. During our 2022 trip, though, things took a turn. We still reacted to cheese plates the way preteens reacted to Harry Styles during the One Direction days (okay fine, the way *I* react to Harry Styles now), but despite the bursts of joy, our weekend trip started to feel a little bit like a vigil.

We were staying in a quiet beach town, in a house drowning in nautical decor. Little anchor figurines served as centerpieces. Sea-green globes suspended inside roped nets hung over the pale blue couch. Two wooden boat paddles were nailed to a wall of shiplap. It was an HGTV-inspired oceanfront dream (or nightmare, depending on your taste). Décor be damned, we were thrilled to be there, together, having our yearly adult slumber party away from kids and jobs and spouses. After we toured the place and settled into our rooms, we poured our glasses of rosé and got cozy on the pale blue couches, surrounded by anchors and ship wheels, symbols of the open sea! This was a stress-free zone. Deep breaths and breezy thoughts happened here. We did relax, but it didn't take long before someone started crying. The sea is powerful, but it can't stop a grown woman from releasing a tidal wave of emotion if she needs to.

"What's wrong," we collectively asked our friend Kerryn, who was the first one to cry that weekend. She would not be the last.

"I'm sorry, I know we're supposed to be having fun, it's just been a lot. It's been a tough year," Kerryn said.

We listened as she told us about her kids leaving for college, her fears of "empty-nest syndrome" (why does every emotion women experience have to be classified as an ailment?), the stresses of her job as a school administrator during a time when school shootings were on everyone's mind. We weren't upset about Kerryn's temporary meltdown. We'd all had them, at various points throughout the year. Now at least we could have them together, in our little nautical-themed cocoon.

Throughout that weekend, the thoughts that weighed on me weighed on them. We had our personal stories, but adding to those were soaring gas prices, drought, news about neofascists detained at a Pride event. Recent shootings in Buffalo, New York, and Uvalde, Texas, and the refusal of our politicians, again, to do anything about it. The imminent reversal of *Roe v. Wade*, monkeypox, inflation, anti-trans legislation, the war in Ukraine, the aftereffects of the pandemic, and the general sense that our country, our world, was utterly doomed. *But wait, look at that cute seashell on the coffee table! It's adorable. Very pretty. Now where were we? Oh, right, the impending apocalypse . . .*

I know that we were lucky to be agonizing over current events in a California beach rental. It's also not as if things have always been incredible for vast swaths of people around the globe, and now, in the twenty-first century, it's suddenly unfair. The world has been both beautiful and cruel since the Cambrian explosion over 540 million years ago. I wasn't around then, but that era has been described as a burst of life that produced "arthropods with legs and compound eyes, worms with feathery gills and swift predators that could crush prey in tooth-rimmed jaws." It sounds horrifically stressful, and eerily familiar. Some days it does feel like swift predators with tooth-rimmed jaws are chasing us all, and we're floating along the bottom of the sea, hoping for just one moment where we don't have to look over our shoulder and panic.

"We need to stop talking about shootings and wildfires. Does anyone have gossip? Maybe we should just talk about gossip or something dumb."

"What about Pete Davidson and Kim Kardashian?"

"PERFECT."

My friends and I didn't really care about Kim and Pete, two celebrities who were inexplicably dating at that time. Maybe they're still dating now. The universe is a baffling mystery. Talking about celebrity couples pulled us out of the verbal and emotional quicksand we kept finding ourselves in throughout that weekend. We were eating Manchego cheese and oysters on a sunny seventy-five-degree day in northern California and looking at farmers' market artichokes the size of footballs, so why in the hell did we keep getting so deep, so dark? Why, as we took photos of bright orange poppies and purple clover, were we talking about hate crimes?

"We should talk about Kim and Pete" became code for *Let's trudge out of this muck and do what we are here to do*, which was to take photos of pretty flowers and have some fucking fun.

Kim and Pete worked for a little while, but there is only so much we had to say about them. We didn't know the intimate details of their lives, so the conversations were limited to comments about the fact that Pete Davidson, who none of us have even been in the same room with, has a type—gorgeous women with long, straight, dark brown hair. That's about as deep as it got, but that was the point.

For each moment that we laughed until we cried watching one friend's old pandemic TikToks, there would be another moment where someone else was actually crying about a parent's declining health. The positive side was that we could do this together. We could have a great time, while also being sad and pissed and blessedly united in our anxiety.

"How did this tradition start?" I asked during that 2022 trip. I couldn't remember when or why we began planning these vacations. We'd spent so many years apart, not making this effort to get together each summer, so what changed? I had no clue.

"Your mom," said Rachel. "It started when we took you away for that weekend trip after your mom died."

My mom, in all her wisdom, brought us back together. She loved these friends, and they each knew and loved her. Maybe this was another sign. My mother was pushing me toward the people I loved and needed most, during the years that weighed heaviest on us all.

Despite the tears and the sighs, I loved that weekend by the sea. When we weren't lamenting crazed dictators, book bans, and the very real possibility that the world as we knew it, as it had always been, was ending, we celebrated. Most likely it was our 1990s go-to, the Pharcyde, that pulled us out of the quicksand and onto the dance floor, also known as the den in our Airbnb. Those moments didn't make me forget that my mom and sister were gone, or that life can feel treacherous and unpredictable, a dark, churning sea, teeming with swift predators. We were fully aware of it all—the joy and the sadness, the tough nights and better days. The sunrise would bring a cool, rainy California morning, so misty the Pacific Ocean would be obscured. Soon enough, we would pack our bags, go our separate ways and head home, but not yet. If we were lucky, we would get another year, another weekend together. On the last night of our stay, in that borrowed room, we did what human beings have done for centuries. We did what Prince beckoned us all to do. Despite any ache in our hearts or sorrow in our bones, we got up onto that makeshift dance floor together. We listened to the music, and let go.

A Few Things
I've Learned about Grief
(in No Particular Order)

- Grief does not discriminate. It is the most open-minded, nonjudgmental state of being on the planet. Anyone and everyone is led past the velvet ropes and into the club. There's no bottle service, no comfortable booths to slip into, and no DJ, so too bad. At least you won't be in there alone.

- If someone says or writes "So sorry for your loss" or "Condolences," they are not lobbing a savage insult your way. They are searching for words of comfort, so accept those words, hold them tight. Anything is better than silence. One exception is "They're in a better place." Another is "Time heals all wounds." Those are offensive. Full stop.

- It's perfectly fine to wear your dad's class ring, take up competitive tablescaping because your sister loved it, or keep your husband's favorite sweater on its hanger for the rest of your life if it makes you feel connected to them. Continuing bonds can be healthy ways to cope with loss, so keep that sweater or that ring as long as you need to.

(And don't judge anyone else for the ways they stay connected. It's personal.)

- Unless you own five yachts and have fifteen Swiss bank accounts, in-home hospice will not resemble a movie, with candlelight, meaningful glances, and nurses on site twenty-four hours a day. It will likely be one of the most challenging experiences of your life. Time will become a melting Salvador Dalí clock. Do not do it alone. Ask for help. Accept help. You are stronger than you think, but you also need to take a nap, brush your teeth, and wash the pajamas you've been wearing for a week straight.

- The famous French philosopher René Descartes was wrong, and Dolly Parton is right (she is *always* right). Dogs have souls, as do cats, rabbits, horses, cows, prairie dogs, and macaws. Mourning their death is nothing to be embarrassed about. If you're mourning a cockroach, fire ant, or a mosquito, though, you should be absolutely mortified.

- You are going to sigh, a lot. There's a certain type of sighing that happens with grief, and it happens every time you think of the person, place, or pet you're missing. It sounds a little like the exhale the instructor asks you to do at the end of a yoga class, times one million. Accepting these deep sighs will help you process your emotions and move past them. Embrace the sigh.

- Hyperventilating is a stage of grief, even though there aren't any concrete "stages" of grief. But if there were, hyperventilating, at least at the beginning, is a thing. Embrace this, too.

- You are not a bad or heartless human if you return to school, work, dating, or the local bowling alley after a loved one dies. Plus, bowling or going on a date might provide a much-needed distraction from your grief. Life will not stop just because you want it to, so, when you're ready, it's there for you to dive back in. Disclaimer: Be prepared for sudden bouts of tears or emotional turmoil (aka the dreaded GIEA) that strike without warning, but do not let them stop you from taking a deep breath and rolling the bowling ball again.

- Climate grief is real, so each time you find yourself freaking out about a dry lake or a story about cows dropping dead from the heat in Kansas, refocus your attention on what's here, what's beautiful, what's good. You can't think about the cows in Kansas forever; it's not healthy.

- Foods that help temporarily alleviate symptoms of grief include buttery mashed potatoes, enchilada casserole, homemade chicken soup, buttery biscuits, chicken potpie, large hunks of pound cake, ramen noodles, chicken and dumplings, and gumbo. You can also bring any of these dishes to bereaved friends, family, or neighbors. Do not bring depressing foods like Melba toast, steamed broccoli, or blanched green beans with zero seasoning. Grief requires butter, salt, flavor, and a whole lot of love.

Recipes That Temporarily Annihilate Feelings of Grief

Blair's Famous Gumbo

One of the first homemade meals we received after my mom died was a huge pot of gumbo from my sister's sister-in-law, Blair. We'd barely eaten during the previous week, and the smell of the spices and the warmth of the dish revived us. Seeing the ingredients makes me even more appreciative, knowing the work that went into this. It's a perfect dish to take to someone in mourning, or to just make for yourself. I know people can get territorial with their gumbo and their roux, so if you feel strongly that something is missing from this recipe, don't yell at me (or at Blair).

Ingredients

1 cup vegetable oil

1 cup all-purpose flour

1 large onion, chopped

1 large green bell pepper, chopped

2 celery stalks, chopped

1 pound andouille or smoked sausage,
   sliced ¼ inch thick

4 cloves garlic, minced

Salt and pepper, to taste

Creole seasoning, to taste

6 cups chicken broth

1 bay leaf

1 rotisserie chicken, boned and shredded

Heat the oil in a Dutch oven or pot over medium heat. When hot, whisk in flour. Continue whisking until the roux has cooked to the color of chocolate milk, 8 to 10 minutes. Be careful not to burn the roux. If you see black specs in the mixture, start over.

Stir onion, bell pepper, celery, and sausage into the roux; cook 5 minutes. Stir in garlic and cook another 5 minutes. Season with salt, pepper, and Creole seasoning; blend thoroughly. Pour in the chicken broth, and add the bay leaf. Bring to a boil over high heat, then reduce heat to medium–low and simmer, uncovered, for 1 hour, stirring occasionally. Stir in the chicken and simmer 1 hour more. Skim off any foam that floats to the top during the last hour.

Serve over rice. And no matter how sad you may feel, eat it up.

My Mom's Famous Chicken Soup

This soup is famous in my family, for good reason. My mom made it when we were kids and walking into the house after school to smell the broth and pepper and chicken she was simmering for us was wildly comforting. It's still comforting, but it also makes me miss my mom and appreciate everything she did for us, like make soup. I add kale to the recipe, which would make my mother turn over in her grave, since she despised kale. It's easy to make, and people can reheat it and eat it for days, which is ideal when someone is grieving. The recipe is based on my mom's instructions: "I don't know exact measurements, honey, I eyeball it." So good luck.

Ingredients

4–5 chicken breasts

Low-sodium chicken broth (just have a bunch of 48-ounce boxes on hand and eyeball it)

Large white onion, cut into pieces (not too small, not too big)

4–5 carrots, peeled and cut into small circles

4–5 celery stalks, cut into small semi-circles

Salt and pepper to taste

A bunch of kale (forgive me, Mom)

A handful of egg noodles (or more, depending on the size of your hand)

Wash and clean the chicken breasts. Pour a bunch of broth into a large pot, until it's about two-thirds full. Add onion, carrots, and celery, and bring to a boil. Add salt and pepper to taste (my mom was generous with the pepper). Add chicken breasts and simmer—maybe 10 minutes. Just pull out the chicken with tongs when it's cooked through, and let it cool. Shred the chicken (don't burn your hands!) and add it back to the pot. Add egg noodles and shredded kale (if you dare), simmer a little while longer until it all tastes perfect.

Serve with hunks of delicious bread.

Suggested Resources

Al-Anon

Offers worldwide recovery and support groups for family and friends of alcoholics.

https://al-anon.org/

Bo's Place

A nonprofit bereavement center located in Houston, Texas. They offer virtual grief groups and counseling, plus online resources.

https://www.bosplace.org/en/

Camp Erin

A national bereavement program for youth and children.

https://elunanetwork.org/camps-programs/camp-erin/

Cancer Care

The largest professionally run nonprofit network of cancer support across the globe.

https://www.cancersupportcommunity.org/

Compassionate Friends

Offers grief support groups across the United States.

https://www.compassionatefriends.org/

Evermore

A nonprofit working to improve bereavement care in America.
https://live-evermore.org/

Open to Hope

An online community that connects people through stories of loss, hope, and recovery.
https://www.opentohope.com/

Shatterproof

An organization dedicated to educating people about addiction and ending the stigma associated with addiction.
https://www.shatterproof.org/

Speaking Grief

A public media initiative, aimed at creating a more grief-aware society.
https://speakinggrief.org/

TAPS

A national support network for those grieving a military friend or loved one.
https://www.taps.org/

Notes

Introduction
page 2: *In a 2019 study about grief and loss . . .*

"Grief: Beyond the 5 Stages," WebMD

https://www.webmd.com/special-reports/grief-stages/20190711
/the-grief-experience-survey-shows-its-complicated.

Chapter 1: This Is Not a Detour
page 14: *What about the fact that . . . an estimated 75 percent of people who have died of Covid in the United States have been sixty-four years old or older*

"Centers for Disease Control and Prevention, Provisional COVID-19 Deaths by Week, Sex, and Age," cited in the *New York Times*

https://www.nytimes.com/2021/12/13/us/covid-deaths-elderly
-americans.html.

Chapter 2: The Long Goodbye
page 38: *An analysis published in the medical journal JAMA . . .*

Kristin E. Knutzen, MPH; Olivia A. Sacks, MD; Olivia C. Brody-Bizar, BA. "Actual and Missed Opportunities for End-of-Life Care Discussions with Oncology Patients," *The Journal of the American Medical Association* 4, no. 6 (2021): e2113193. Doi:10.1001 (2021)

https://jamanetwork.com/journals/jamanetworkopen/fullarticle
/2780865?widget=personalizedcontent&previousarticle
=2785790file:///Users/smcbride/Downloads/knutzen_2021_oi
_210394_1622663607.3491.pdf.

Chapter 2: The Long Goodbye
page 49: *A 2017 study conducted by the Kaiser Family Foundation (KFF) and The Economist . . .*

Liz Hamel, Brian Wu, and Mollyann Brodie, "Views and Experiences with End of Life Medical Care in the U.S.," Kaiser Family Foundation (2017)

https://www.kff.org/other/report/views-and-experiences-with-end-of-life-medical-care-in-the-u-s/.

Chapter 2: The Long Goodbye
page 50: *Dr. Melissa Wachterman, a palliative care physician at Harvard Medical School . . .*

Melissa W. Wachterman, M.D., M.P.H.; Elizabeth A. Luth, Ph.D.; Robert S. Semco, B.S.E.; and Joel S. Weissman, Ph.D., "Where Americans Die—Is There Really No Place Like Home?" *New England Journal of Medicine* (March 17, 2022)

https://www.nejm.org/doi/full/10.1056/NEJMp2112297.

Chapter 5: It's a Sign
page 90: *The mirror now sits on display at the British Museum . . .*

Stuart Campbell, Elizabeth Healey, Yaroslav Juzman, and Michael D. Glascock, "The Mirror, the Magus and More: Reflections on John Dee's Obsidian Mirror," Cambridge University Press (October 7, 2021)

https://www.cambridge.org/core/journals/antiquity/article/mirror-the-magus-and-more-reflections-on-john-dees-obsidian-mirror/38D4BFEA2CB9766973791029C2EE1289.

Chapter 5: It's a Sign
page 92: *A 2013 study published in the Journals of Gerontology* . . .

Deborah Carr and Shane Sharp, "Do Afterlife Beliefs Affect Psychological Adjustment to Late-Life Spousal Loss?," *Journals of Gerontology*, Series B, 69B, Issue 1 (January 2014): 103–112 https://doi.org/10.1093/geronb/gbt063.

Chapter 5: It's a Sign
page 98: *A study of Japanese widows* . . .

Joe Yamamoto, Keigo Okonogi, Tetsuya Iwasaki, and Saburo Yoshimura, "Mourning in Japan," *American Journal of Psychiatry* (April 1, 2006) https://ajp.psychiatryonline.org/doi/abs/10.1176/ajp.125.12.1660.

Chapter 6: Telling My "Safe Place" to Go to Hell
page 108: *In a 2011 study, conducted by researchers at the University of Texas at Austin and the University of Minnesota* . . .

Arthur Markman, Todd Maddox, Kathleen Vohs, and Brian Glass, "Social Psychological and Personality Science" (March 24, 2011) https://news.utexas.edu/2011/03/23/psychologists-find-the -meaning-of-aggression/.

Chapter 7: Mourning Them When They're Here, But Not
page 126: *It is estimated that 95,000 people in America die from alcohol-related causes annually.* . . .

National Institute on Alcohol Abuse and Alcoholism https://www.niaaa.nih.gov/publications/brochures-and -fact-sheets/alcohol-facts-and-statistics#:~:text=An%20 estimated%2095%2C000%20people%20.

Chapter 8: *J'aime Mon Chien*
page 153: *A 2020 study by researchers at Massachusetts General Hospital found that, for children . . .*

K. M. Crawford, Y. Zhu, K. A. Davis, "The Mental Health Effects of Pet Death during Childhood: Is It Better to Have Loved and Lost Than Never to Have Loved at All?" *European Child & Adolescent Psychiatry* 30 (2021): 1547–1558 https://doi.org/10.1007/s00787-020-01594-5.

Chapter 10: 'Til Death Do Us Part (Please Wear Sunscreen and Get a Colonoscopy)
page 184: *A 2006 study, published in the New England Journal of Medicine . . .*

Nicholas A. Christakis, M.D., Ph.D., M.P.H., and Paul D. Allison, Ph.D., "Mortality after Hospitalization of a Spouse," *New England Journal of Medicine* 354 (February 16, 2006): 719–730. Doi: 10.1056/NEJMsa050196 https://www.nejm.org/doi/full/10.1056/nejmsa050196.

Chapter 10: 'Til Death Do Us Part (Please Wear Sunscreen and Get a Colonoscopy)
page 184: *Another study, published in 2013 in the Journal of Public Health . . .*

J. Robin Moon, M. Maria Glymour, Anusha M. Vable, Sze Y. Liu, and S. V. Subramanian, "Short- and Long-Term Associations between Widowhood and Mortality in the United States: Longitudinal Analyses," *Journal of Public Health* 36, Issue 3 (September 2014): 382–389 https://doi.org/10.1093/pubmed/fdt101 https://academic.oup.com/jpubhealth/article/36/3/382/1521696?login=false.

Acknowledgments

During the course of writing this book, so many incredible people shared their stories of loss and grief, stories that will stay with me forever. Thank you to the therapists, counselors, psychologists, and experts who took the time to provide insight and guidance. The work you do every day helps us all face the often conflicting emotions we're dealing with, and opens up conversations that will hopefully reverse the stigma of making loss part of our everyday lives, and help us all find comfort in remembrance.

To the parents, children, siblings, friends, and partners mourning loved ones, who trusted me with some of the toughest moments you've experienced. Your courage helped me become a little braver, and your commitment to accepting grief into your lives reminds me to work, each day, to do the same.

To everyone at Union Square & Co. who believed in this book, and gave it a home. To Kate Zimmermann, who embraced this project from the beginning and gave me a reason to dance around the living room when I got the good news. To my editor, Jessica Firger, whose clear-eyed, thoughtful, sensitive notes pushed me to go deeper and try harder, even when I thought writing about grief for months on end had sucked me dry and I didn't have anything left. This book would not be what it is without you, and I'm forever thankful for your guidance.

To everyone at UTA and my main squeeze there, my agent Brandi Bowles. For almost ten years, you have been right there by my side, on every phone call and every endless email chain. You've cheered me on through it all, and I'm so grateful to have you on this wild ride with me. Thank you for always bringing the honesty, and for being patient when I am not (which is often). Thank you for being there when I lost my mom, and then my sister, and for being a trusted friend, always.

To the friends who text me during red carpets, whisk me away on much-needed "girls' trips," and engage in years-long text chains about anything and everything. I adore you.

For Jerett, who listened to me talk about grief, death, and loss every day for a year. Your presence has steadied me at funerals, and comforted me when I randomly burst into tears because I'm thinking about my mom or Jackie. Thank you for putting Cole to bed all those nights I stayed up late "tinkering" with this book. I love you, and please keep putting on sunscreen.

For my sweet Cole. Thank you for always keeping me laughing, and for filling me with joy through all the tough times. I hope one day when you're old enough to read this book, you'll get to know your Cici and Aunt Jackie a little bit. They loved you so much, and always will.

To Dad. You are the only person in the world who could make me feel safe jumping off a sixteen-foot dock into a lake by saying, "Just focus on me." How did we get so lucky with you? You opened your heart to me countless times when I would text in the middle of a workday and say, "Dad, can I ask you a few more questions for the book?" Thank you for letting me tell our story, your story. Thank you for being vulnerable, for walking by our side through this life, and for giving us the gift of your sweetness, your humanity, and your love.

To my baby sisters, Amy and Kathryn. Our bond will never be broken, and we will always be four. Thank you for always being the ones I can call, crying, or laughing, or complaining, or all three at once. I won the sister lotto with you both, and I love you more.

Finally, to anyone who has experienced deep loss. My heart is with you, always.

About the Author

(photo: Jessica Comiskey)

Dina Gachman is a Pulitzer Center Grantee and a frequent contributor to the *New York Times*, *Vox*, *Teen Vogue*, *Texas Monthly*, and more. She's a *New York Times* bestselling ghostwriter, and the author of *Brokenomics: 50 Ways to Live the Dream on a Dime*. Her essay "Marriage, Love and IVF after 40" was selected to appear in the L.A. Times book *L.A. Affairs*. She lives near Austin, Texas, with her husband, son, and dog.

Walking under the oaks after hospice